After 3PM

AFTER 3PM

Asking the question: "Why do teachers have unlawful relationships with students?" …by a teacher who did

KURT MICHAEL BRUNDAGE

NEW YORK

LONDON • NASHVILLE • MELBOURNE • VANCOUVER

AFTER 3PM

Asking the question: "Why do teachers have unlawful relationships with students?" …by a teacher who did

Published in New York, New York, by Morgan James Publishing. Morgan James is a trademark of Morgan James, LLC. www.MorganJamesPublishing.com

The Morgan James Speakers Group can bring authors to your live event. For more information or to book an event visit The Morgan James Speakers Group at www.TheMorganJamesSpeakersGroup.com.

ISBN 9781683506836 paperback
ISBN 9781683506843 eBook
Library of Congress Control Number: 2017911619

Cover Design by:
Megan Whitney
megan@creativeninjadesigns.com

Interior Design by:
Chris Treccani
www.3dogcreative.net

In an effort to support local communities, raise awareness and funds, Morgan James Publishing donates a percentage of all book sales for the life of each book to Habitat for Humanity Peninsula and Greater Williamsburg.

Get involved today! Visit
www.MorganJamesBuilds.com

This book is dedicated to those who never gave up on me,
even after I'd given up on myself.

CONTENTS

PREFACE

The epidemic of teacher-student relationships is eating away at the bedrock of the American educational system, and it is an epidemic which is not being sufficiently addressed. Any half-effort attempts at merely acknowledging the problem are overshadowed by the numerous instances of ineffectiveness proven by the repeated news stories of the latest teacher charged with some manner of sexual misconduct with a student.

However, this book does not seek to answer the questions surrounding why certain teachers are sexual deviants. Teachers arrested for child pornography and sexual exploitation, or teachers who are arrested for abusing children in elementary school — these teachers aren't in the same ballpark as those to which I refer. Teachers who prey on small prepubescent children, or who seek pictures and videos of these children are sick predators who deserve every single second of prison time they receive. So, I will not even attempt to pry into the demented mind of someone who is attracted to elementary-age children. That is an entirely separate pathology which I'm not sure I even want to understand.

Listen: My choices were *not* the fault of the school administration or a lack of training. My choices were *not* the fault of my universities or a lack of education. My choices were *not* the fault of my personal struggles or my lack of happiness.

PURPOSE

This isn't just a book about the issue, and this is *not* a book about my crime. This is a book about *all* aspects of the experience — and how to fix it.

My aim is to provide a clear understanding of why teachers — typically high school teachers — reach a point in their own cognitive distortions when they think it is permissible to carry on an adult-like emotional and/or sexual relationship with students ranging from ages 14 to 18. In many states, there is a legal line drawn at age thirteen regarding the severity of charges filed against a perpetrator. For example, in Kansas, sexual crimes against someone under the age of thirteen is a more severe classification than someone between the ages of fourteen and seventeen. And if a teacher has a sexual relationship with a student who is eighteen-years-old, it is still against the law, a crime classified as *Unlawful Sexual Relations.*[1]

There are two dominating questions regarding this issue that have not been sufficiently addressed:

"Why is this happening?"

"What can prevent this?"

I am asking these questions from a very personal and unique perspective; I was one of those teachers. In 2010, I had a brief relationship with a former student who was fifteen at the time; and in

---

1   This is the same criminal classification given to sexual crimes by prison guards, for example.

2012, I was arrested and sent to prison for more than two years. But this book is not about me or my crime. This book is about the overall issue — I am simply bringing a new and unique perspective to the conversation.

Or, perhaps, I am attempting to *start* a conversation. In just a few short years, my own daughter will be entering high school. And knowing what *actually* goes on in high schools — around corners, in shadows, and behind closed doors — it scares me a little that there are still teachers teaching who are conducting themselves just as I did. Actually, it scares me *a lot*.

Nothing justifies what these teachers — we teachers — have done. And yet, I do not seek to demonize these teachers, but to understand them. Nothing can be said to lessen the tragic and traumatic impact this sort of conduct has on students. I do not stand-up for these teachers, nor do I defend my own actions. *There is no defense.*

I am merely asking the simple (yet complex) question: *Why?*

My choices were *my choices*. I don't blame *anyone* except *me*. I did *not* make the choices I made simply because I was never told not to what I did. I did *not* make the choices I made because I was a sick deviant who sought-out intimacy with an underage girl. The fact is, it took me several years to understand why I made the choices I made, but in the end, I discovered I was asking the wrong question. The question I was asking was, "Why did I make the choices I made?" However, the question I should have been asking was "Why did I think the choices I made were acceptable?" At first glance, they seem to mean the same thing, but in reality, they could not be more different.

At no point to do I seek to minimize or justify my choices or behaviors.[2] At 100% of the time, I was 100% in the wrong. So, do not

---

2   I cannot emphasize this enough. The biggest struggle I've faced ever since I embarked on this endeavor has been the repeated accusations and mockery from people who seem to perceive this as my own grandiose way of somehow trying to justify what I did or minimize my own level of responsibility in the choices I made. But I have come to learn that those individuals will never be receptive to this message because they only want to point their fingers at offenders, not open their minds to new ideas or results. It's "more comfortable" to point fingers than it is to open minds. Thus, if you are of the

view my perspective as, "What could have prevented me from making these choices?" Instead, view it as, "How can the perspective of this issue change to prevent it from happening in the future?" I am not trying to justify how my actions could have been prevented; I am trying to change the conversation entirely, to see it differently, to perceive it differently, to address it differently, to approach it differently.

Writing this book forced me to take a very difficult journey, coming face-to-face with many of my own demons. And while I am conscious of the choices I made, the terrible things I did, and the lasting impacts my choices have on others, I am also thankful for my time in prison. Prison was the jolt I needed to get my head on straight and correct my way of thinking.

The purpose of this book has very little to do with the relationship I had with my former student — it will serve as an anecdote and a narrative. My hope is to bring a depth of reality to the issue beyond the limited details of my crime released by the news media by giving deeper details and making it more "real." Details and dialogue tend to do that. I do not include the specifics of my own transgressions for any purpose other than to add a depth of understanding to what a person truly experiences when these choices are made and these processes are put into motion. Most (if not all) of the details I recount are things for which I will always feel shame and embarrassment.

Therefore, for the purposes of these writings, the student with whom I had the relationship will be referred to as "Taissa."[3] This is obviously not her real name, and although public court documents identify her only as "RLF," I have decided to refrain from identifying her in this narrative by her actual name as a matter of privacy to her.

---

opinion that I will spend nearly 70,000 words trying to justify what I did, please stop reading this book. Return it to the bookstore. I hope you saved your receipt. Because in order to fully grasp my purpose, you need to think outside the box with an open mind, not with extended accusatory fingers. Sometimes, the bad guy knows how to solve the crime.

3   I chose this alias simply because she is the literal doppelganger of Taissa Farmiga, known for her role in *American Horror Story*.

This is a book about why teachers in these situations make the choices we make and what can be done within the school systems to shed light upon this issue with the goal of preventing instances of teacher-student relationships in the future.

This is not a book about my crime; this is an in-depth narrative about how these situations emerge, what happens when these situations are discovered, the aftermath of these situations, and the truth about why this epidemic continues to plague the educational community.

Unfortunately, teachers and school administrators both struggle with the same problem: They have no idea what the *actual* problem is or how to *actually* fix it; they only see the result, the aftermath, and the damage.

It is time to stop merely treating the symptoms and, instead, cure the underlying disease.

Essentially, the problem is not simply that teacher and students are having inappropriate relationships. That is merely the result. The problem is much deeper, much more complex, and much more obvious than anyone wants to admit.

Every high school teacher and principal should read this book, not because everyone is at risk of having a relationship with a student; instead, everyone needs to know which battles to fight and how to fight them — which warning signs to see, and how to see them — which teachers to catch and how to catch them.

The time for depending on "individual responsibility" on this issue has long passed. A concerted effort by the entire faculty of every school must be put forth, because there is one simple fact which teachers and principals tend to overlook: The teachers they see on the news are simply the teachers who got caught.

PERSPECTIVE

This particularly unique perspective is necessary. Teachers see disgraced educators like me on television, shake their heads at our horrid choices, hear that we are going to prison, and then never hear from us again. Out-of-sight, out-of-mind. So, another purpose of this book is to provide a glimpse into what happens to disgraced teachers when we aren't the top news story anymore; sent to prison, released from prison, forced to live in the shadows of humiliation and shame. I use my own narrative[4] experience as an eye-opening example of what happens to a teacher, both before the news story airs and after it has faded into the archives.

People see these teachers — *us* teachers — who have done these horrible things, featured across the many spectrums of the news and Internet in the latest scandal that rocks the educational community of "Anytown, USA." People point fingers and say things like "sick" or "horrible" or "pervert" or "pedophile" or any number of words aimed at degrading a teacher for choosing to pursue a relationship with a student. And yet, with all the social backlash and humiliation, these instances do not decrease — in fact, they are on the rise. Teachers increasingly continue to cross the lines of propriety and legality with their students.

---

4   Fair warning: I overuse the word "seriously;" I begin far too many sentences with the words "And" or "But" or "Because;" I write long sentences; there are hundreds of footnotes; I tend to bend the rules on the uses of the dash and semicolon; and I love to quote people (real and fictional).

But therein lies the crux of my philosophy: People see only what they want to see, and then they forget — they move on. When I was arrested and sent to prison, I was actually thankful for the fast-paced twenty-four-hour news cycle because it meant my face would be off the news and would fade into obscurity relatively quickly. I was held up for humiliation for a day or two when I was arrested, and then for a day or two when I was sentenced, and that was it. Even my former colleagues probably never give me a second thought anymore.[5]

Disgraced teachers are seen on the news, in court, and then being led off to prison, and that's it — on to the next news story. But what happens after the cameras are off? What happens when the top story becomes old news — after the humiliation, after the sentencing, after prison? The story dies, but the person must live on — the person must pick up the pieces and try to reassemble something resembling normality, often with little (or no) success. And it has been my experience that life after the news — life after prison — has been more difficult than standing in front of a judge, surrounded by news cameras, admitting that I'd had a relationship with a fifteen-year-old former student.

This is what teachers need to see; *this* is what teachers need to hear. Teachers need to see what happens, not just when they are arrested, convicted, and sent to prison; teachers need to see what it's like to re-enter the world, knowing they cannot — *ever* — be a teacher again. That is the reality in which I now exist.

Look at me. *Look hard.*

This is what a ruined life looks like.[6]

---

5   Although, in the years following my release from prison, I've encountered several former colleagues and students, and those encounters have been overwhelmingly positive.

6   Granted, it could be worse. Am I doing life in prison? No, I'm doing life outside of prison. The life I had (as a respected educator and valued member of society) is gone, never to be returned. The life I live now (as a convicted felon, a sex offender, and a humiliated individual) is the truth of my existence. I don't expect anyone who has not been through this to fully understand my point here, and I hope no one ever has to either. So here's my point: This is what a ruined life looks like, and I sincerely hope you never have to understand how or why.

> *The darkest places in hell are reserved for those who maintain their neutrality in times of moral crisis.*

-Dante Alighieri

Inferno

PROLOGUE

Deep in the rural woodlands of South Carolina, Cypress Gardens Boat Landing sits next to the glass-smooth waters of Chicken Creek. The tall narrow trees surrounding the aging wooden docks reach to the heavens toward the sun, like the arms of a singing congregation reaching toward a merciful God. The still lily pads on the creek's surface sit calmly, only moving with a gentle sway in the wake of a passing canoe or rowboat. The water seems green, but only because it reflects the beauty of the trees and foliage embracing it. It is a landscape of serene and quiet peace — the kind of place for a first date, a first kiss, proposals, or wedding vows — "like something out of a Robert Frost poem."

In the long post-sunrise moments of Wednesday, August 24, 2016, high school teacher Donald Blair sat on the docks of Cypress Gardens Boat Landing. The late summer had given way to an early morning coolness, rolling freely from the air above the water onto the docks that reached beyond the shore. And as Don sat motionless, breathing in this fresh morning breeze, he held two things: the deepest remorse for the choices he'd made, and the handle of his .45 caliber handgun.

There was a stillness in the air, as though time had stopped. The water stood motionless beneath the dock, like a giant mirror reflecting the pale-blue morning heavens. The air smelled dewy and fresh like a lavender-scented candle, but the taste in his mouth was entirely different. His tongue was bitter and cold, smothered by the metallic taste of the barrel of his gun.

At the very moment he sat on that dock, he was fully aware that he was expected elsewhere. Don knew there was a group of school district officials waiting for him in a conference room at the district office. He knew he was missing this meeting, but he couldn't bring himself to show his face. The shame, the humiliation, the failure was too much. He simply could not bring himself to make the drive to that building and see those people, knowing what he'd done.

In the silence, Don could hear the screams in his head, the ridicules and insults hurled at him online from anonymous Internet comments, calling him a pedophile, a pervert, a rapist, and calling for his swift and prompt execution on the front lawn of the school. Two days earlier, Don was sitting in the Berkeley County Jail, arrested for having a sexual relationship with a 15-year-old student nearly two years prior.

In a way, he knew this was coming. Only a few weeks earlier, he watched the news as a former assistant principal at the same school was sentenced to five years in jail for a nearly identical crime. So, in the back of his mind, Don knew he would eventually be next.

As he sat on the dock, surrounded by the calming natural beauty of the woods and the motionless flow of the water in Chicken Creek, Don's heart raced uncontrollably. His breathing was deep and rapid. His thoughts were fleeting. He asked himself how he could have made the choices he made. He asked himself why he thought it would be permissible to have sex with a 15-year-old student at the school. He asked why he didn't learn from the dozens upon dozens of cases identical to his which he'd seen on the news, stories of teachers arrested for having relationships with their students. He asked himself what would happen to his life now.

He had no answers.

He had no hope.

So, in an instance of misshapen chaos of well-seeming forms, Donald Blair did the only thing he could think of that would make any sense whatsoever to anyone, including himself.

Donald Blair pulled the trigger.

Justice.

CHAPTER ONE

During the mildly chilly days in early March of 2012 — at about
that time of year when Kansas can't decide if it wants to hold
onto the chills of winter for just a bit longer or usher-in the
rebirth of spring — I was a small-town high school English teacher.
It was my sixth year as a teacher, my first at that particular school.
The five years prior, starting in 2006, I taught at the largest high
school in the state, which also happened to be my alma mater. But
as wonderful as it was to teach at my own high school, I'd managed
to completely ruin it for myself. I'd managed to have multiple (often
overlapping) affairs with various women on the faculty, carrying-on
sexual escapades both in the school building and elsewhere. Then, in
2010 I had a brief (four-week) relationship with a former student.
No one knew except the two of us, but the experience was enough to
convince me that I was completely out of control.

It is difficult to describe the out-of-control life I was leading,
especially since I seemed to be so accomplished at keeping it a secret.
But essentially, I exhibited no sense of morality, honesty, fidelity, or
ethics (which is one reason I fit-in so well with some of my colleagues).
But after having affair after affair with so many women, and finally
crossing the line with a former student, I simply could not live that

1

life anymore. So I decided to confess. I would confess everything to my wife — every affair, every woman, every cheating instance in which I failed her as a husband, including the brief fling with the former student.

Confession

One night, after our daughter was asleep, my wife and I sat down together in my home-office, and I began the painful task of telling my wife how I betrayed her. The secrets I kept were acid inside my soul, eating away at me from the inside. Oddly, I didn't really feel much guilt about the affairs I was having with my colleagues until I crossed the teacher-student line. It honestly scared me that I was capable of doing such a thing and it was enough to force all my cards onto the table.

"First, I want you to know that I love you, I'm *in* love with you, and you are the best thing that has ever happened to me," I said, never breaking eye contact, clutching both of her hands as we sat knee-to-knee.

"I know," she replied, "and I love you too. Nothing you could say would ever change that." I wasn't sure if she would be able to hold to that after I told her what I had to say.

"Remember my former student, Taissa?"

"Yes," she replied, and I was quite confident that she knew where this conversation was going.

"Lately, you and I haven't been getting along, and I'm always gone, and I sleep on the couch a lot of nights; you know what I mean?"

She nodded.

"Well," I went on, "Taissa has been coming to see me in my classroom quite a bit, almost every day. And I've seen her outside of school a few times too."

I paused, trying to read her body language and facial expression, but she just kept looking at me, no looks of disappointment or anger, even though I was sure she knew what I was going to say next.

"Since I've been seeing Taissa," I took a deep breath, "*things* have happened."

She nodded again, not as if to say, *How could you do this to me?* but rather, it was as though she was saying, *Are you okay?*

I expected her to say, "Things?" or "Like what?" But she remained silent.

I continued. "I didn't sleep with her, okay? We *did not* have sex. I promise."[7] And with that, she lightly exhibited her first sign of emotion: Relief. Her shoulders rested a little and her face seemed to relax.

"It's *over*, though, and I can't go any further without being honest with you about what I've done and beg for your forgiveness. You're my wife, and I betrayed your love and your trust." I paused, hoping for an answer, and finally, she spoke.

"You're my husband, and I love you, for *better* or for *worse*," she said confidently. "We will get through this." And then she said something I will never forget. "I did not marry you to divorce you." She spoke with subtle authority as though she were making a point she wanted me to remember for the rest of my life — and I have.

A weight lifted. I knew she loved me, but as she looked into my eyes, I genuinely knew how much. Before we began talking, I was ready to do whatever I needed to do to comfort her once I'd confessed my betrayal, but instead, she wanted to comfort me. She saw the pain I was in, and wanted to make *me* feel better.

I could honestly see the love of God in my wife — in how she handled the news, and how she was immediately willing to forgive me. I just hoped her forgiveness would continue.

"There's more," I said, my voice stammering and quivering.

When I was done talking about Taissa, I told her about the history teacher, and then the psychology teacher, and then the English teacher, and then the elementary teacher, and on and on and on, back as far (and as many) as I could remember, finishing with the very first time

---

7   This statement is 100% true.

I cheated, four months after we got married, with a woman I met at a bar, while my wife was pregnant with our daughter.

I'd never felt so low in my entire life.

She cried a little. I cried a lot. We cried together. And when my confessions finally concluded, I asked her, very delicately, for her thoughts.

"I need to know what you're thinking," I said. "If you want me out of here tonight, I'll go stay with one of my buddies."[8]

"Well," she said, drying her eyes, "no, you're staying here tonight." She looked up and made eye contact with me in a way that she never had before, and in a way that I will never — *ever* — forget. "I didn't marry you to divorce you," she said again in a stern voice. "For *better* or *worse*, till death do us part."

After confessing everything — and I mean *everything* — to my wife, we decided it would be wise to relocate and start over. In the summer of 2011, I finished graduate school

and we left; we moved away to a new town, I got a job at a new school, and we began embarking on our new life.

During the subsequent spring semester at my new school, in March of 2012, the weather was still bitter cold, showing little potential for allowing Spring to blossom. Basketball season had just ended, and the mid-point grind of the semester curriculum was in full-swing. I was teaching senior and sophomore English and doing well — actually, doing the best I'd ever done. I was enjoying the simple fact that I was teaching at a school without having any affairs with any teachers and without having any questionable student interactions. I was at a new school, I felt like a new teacher, I felt like a new person, and I was finally doing things the right way. I'd made some horrid choices before, but as I taught that year, there was a blissful calm in my demeanor as I took comfort in knowing I was finally doing the right thing.

Leaving town was easy, actually. There were so many skeletons in my hometown from my checkered past that it was a genuine relief

---

8   None of whom talk to me anymore. Go figure.

to envision having a fresh start. Moving away felt like my first real opportunity to put the past behind me and begin the life I'd always known I should have been living. It seemed as if my hometown harbored a dark memory around every corner and in every shadow, hiding and revealing things I regretted as well as things which regretfully happened to me. So, walking away was the easy part.

A Phone Call

However, my blissful calm was shattered by one, single, solitary phone call. Taissa, the former student with whom I'd had the brief relationship, had sent me a message out-of-the-blue through social media which simply read, "Hey... There are some things I really need to talk to you about, but I don't get on my facebook very often anymore...[9] Can you send me your cell number?"

My heart felt like it stopped. I felt paralyzed, scared, confused. I didn't know what to think. All I knew was that I'd spent so much time in prayer, filled with regret over what had happened between the two of us, and I didn't know how to respond. But I immediately wrote back and gave her my phone number and eagerly awaited her call, not because I wanted to talk to her, but because I wanted to know why she wanted to talk to me. The uncertainty filled me with a sense of anxiety that I had never felt before.

I waited and waited that night for a call that never came. From my iPhone, I wrote back several times on Facebook. "Is everything okay? You can call now if you want." Nothing. "Or text? You've got me a bit worried." Still nothing. I wrote back the next day, "Still want to talk? Hoping to hear from you…" And again, nothing.

For days, I received nothing from her. I wrote again two days later, "Please call or text. I would like to talk as well. I would really appreciate it. Sorry for the messages, but thank you for your initial willingness to talk."

---

9   A lie.

It wasn't until five days after her first message that she finally wrote back on Facebook, "Sorry, as I said I don't get on my facebook often,[10] and my mom has access to see it and is a little suspicious,[11] but I'm just keeping things on the down low. I get off work around 3 and I'm going to go grab something to eat and I will call you around 3:30."

Then, at around 3:40, she called me.

I answered.[12]

"Hello?" I could feel my voice trembling

"Hi, it's Taissa," she said, sounding chipper.

"How are you?" I asked.

"I'm good. Just graduated, going to WSU now," she said.

Something didn't seem right.

"What's up?" I asked.

"I was just wondering if you were going to be back in Wichita soon. I really want to talk about . . . everything," she said.

"Yes," I began, "I can come back next weekend if you want. I would really like the chance to talk about this because I've put so much thought and prayer into this."[13]

"Yeah?" she said, sounding more disingenuous.

"Yeah," I replied, "I've just thought a lot about the things we've done and the consequences of everything and how much it scares me and—" I rambled on for several minutes, and she said nothing. And as I was talking, I asked myself, *Why is she just letting me talk like this? Unless, this is being recorded. Oh—sh*t!*[14] I stopped talking and

---

10   Another lie.

11   And another lie. But, you know, whatever.

12   The following conversation is not a perfect word-for-word recollection of the dialogue. It is how I remember it. But the police department refused to give me a copy of the actual transcript, so this is the best I can do.

13   ...not that it did any good.

14   I may or may not have said this out-loud. Check the transcript.

listened as the silence told me everything. I knew, then-and-there, it was a set-up. I didn't want to believe it, but I was nearly certain.

She let me talk and talk and ramble on-and-on, so that whichever cop was on the other side of the line with her could document everything, hoping I'd spill into a confession by discussing our relationship over the phone. And though I never said anything directly incriminating during that phone call, I would have had trouble explaining away, in court, many of the allusions I made to "things" or "stuff" that "happened" several years prior.

I let her take control of the conversation. She suggested that on the evening I returned to town, Friday night, we should meet at a small diner to have dinner and talk things through. I agreed.

I went home and told my wife everything that had transpired.

"That former student, Taissa," I told her, "wants me to come see her on Friday night because she says she wants to talk about everything that happened." My wife's first reaction to this was positive.

"Well, that's a good thing," she said. "You've been wanting to apologize for a long time, and now you'll have your chance."

"Or," I said, bringing her, and myself, back to reality, "this is all a ploy to get me back to Wichita so they can arrest me for the stuff she and I did together two years ago."

"I doubt it," she said, still smiling. "That seems like a lot just to get you back to town."

"You'd think," I replied, "but if the local police here just came and arrested me, then they'd have to extradite me back there, and they'd have to pay for the transportation and everything. These cheap people aren't going to do that when they can just exploit Taissa to get me to come right to them."[15]

"Well, still," she said, "I think this is a good thing." She smiled again. "This is one more way we can put your past behind you."

---

15   I've always thought this was kind of a shady move on the part of the Wichita Police. I mean, seriously, who uses the victim of a crime like this as bait to get the perpetrator to simply come back, just to save a few bucks on transportation costs? You stay classy, Mr. Detective.

"I hope so," I replied with a shallow smile.

But I was pretty sure I knew better.

The Last Day

That Friday was my last day as a teacher. I didn't consciously know it at the time, but I'm reasonably certain I subconsciously knew. I remember feeling a sentimental sense of finality as the day wore on, like a subtle and silent farewell to the job, the career, and the life I'd grown to love.

I think I smiled a little more that day. I think I laughed a little more that day. I think I enjoyed being a teacher a little more that day because deep-down I knew it was over — not because I was happy not to be teaching anymore, but rather because I wanted my last day as a teacher to be a happy one. And I remember, as I walked out of my classroom on that Friday, flipping the lights off and pushing the door open into the empty hallway, I paused.

I turned and looked back into my dark classroom, illuminated only by the natural light which crept in from the half-blinded windows. I looked back and I remembered how I'd gotten there — not simply gotten to be a teacher at that school, but how I'd gotten to be a teacher in general, six years earlier. I remembered what it was like to be a first-year teacher, before I ruined everything. I remembered how it felt to stand in front of a class for the first time, before I ruined everything. I remembered how it felt to dismiss my last class of the day, before I ruined everything. I remembered how it always *should have* felt to be a teacher, before I ruined everything. And with a deep longing breath, I took a step into the hallway, giving my classroom one last glance before the door shut behind me with a thud and clasp of finality. It would be the last time I would set foot in a classroom — *any* classroom — ever.

That evening my wife, my six-year-old daughter, and I packed a weekend's-worth of clothes and made the two-hour drive to Wichita.[16]

---

16   The longest drive of my life.

We told our daughter that we were going to go visit Grandma and Granddad for the weekend, and this always excited her. The whole drive, she talked about how much fun the weekend would be; my wife kept giving me looks of comfort, hoping I would relax, but I was a complete and utterly-nervous wreck. She was confident that everything would be okay; I had no such confidence.

When we finally pulled up in my parents' driveway, our daughter hopped out and ran and gave my dad a hug. I got out but didn't leave the car because I was going to go straight to where Taissa wanted me to meet her. My wife came around to my side of the car, gave me a kiss and a long hug, and told me everything was going to be okay.

"I hope so," I replied, "but if you don't get a text message from me in a half-an-hour, I've been arrested."

"Stop," she said. "That's not going to happen," and she kissed me again.

"I hope you're right," I said. But I knew better.

Driving away from my wife that night, glancing back in the rearview mirror as she strolled into my dad's house, I found myself wishing I could be as faithful and forgiving as she had always been. But I also knew, if this "dinner" with Taissa didn't go well, I may never see my wife again, or worse yet, she may never want to see me again. And the worst part of all was knowing, in all of this, tangled between a cheating husband, a forgiving wife, and an unlawful relationship, was my innocent and naïve six-year-old daughter.

After driving a few blocks, I called Taissa's cell phone to let her know I was on my way.

"I'll be there in about ten minutes," I said to her.

"Okay," she replied. "But, hey," she quickly interjected, "my car won't be at the restaurant. I'm driving my brother's car. Mine is in the shop."

"Okay," I replied. And with that, I *knew* it was a set-up. She needed to give me an excuse for why her car wouldn't be in the parking lot.

That told me all I needed to know. I knew I'd be going to jail that night.[17]

I pulled up to the restaurant, got out, and walked toward the front door.

I took perhaps a dozen steps between my car and that door, and they would be the last steps I took in the world as I'd known it for thirty-two years.

Everything was about to change.

---

17   Over the years, more than a few people have asked me, if I knew it would be a set-up and I was going to be arrested, why did I continue to the restaurant? And the answer is simple. If they had enough on me to con and lure me into a place where they could arrest me, then it really wouldn't have mattered. Either I went to them or they came to me. And I would much rather be arrested in front of a bunch of trashy people at this C-grade restaurant than in my own home in front of my family, and my daughter.

CHAPTER TWO

During life's moments when everything changes in a single instant, that instant seems to last for a tremendously long amount of time, like that scene in *The Matrix* when time suddenly slows down and the distorted trail of the bullets can be seen. There is a surreal sense of uneasiness which chills the blood and accelerates the heart; sudden subtle moments of light-headedness coupled with a dizzying sense of fast-paced slow motion. "Misshapen chaos of well-seeming forms."

Time stops.

Arrested

Indeed, everything was about to change.

Before I could open the front door of the restaurant, it swung open on its own and the mammoth human stepped through the doorway in front of me wearing a badge that read *Wichita Police Department*.

"Are you Kurt?" he asked. But I didn't feel as if this question actually necessitated an answer. I just dropped my head and stared blankly at the ground as he placed his hands on my shoulders, turned me around, and began to tighten a pair of cold metal handcuffs around my wrists.

Within seconds of the final click of those iron bracelets, no fewer than three police cars appeared in the parking lot.[18] One pulled-up directly in front of me, and I was leaned over the trunk and given a very thorough pat-search. My car was also searched; my cell phone and laptop computer were seized as evidence.

I never did see Taissa.[19]

I was promptly squeezed into the backseat[20] of a police car and driven away. The two officers in the car who were escorting me away from my freedom — from life as I knew it — attempted to make small-talk with me as I sat uncomfortably handcuffed in their shoebox-sized backseat, and I did my best to oblige. They asked me about my favorite sports team and the unseasonably cool weather and the drive from Lawrence to Wichita; it struck me as a little out-of-place considering my life had practically just ended and I was still moderately in shock, even if I did see this coming and knew exactly what was going to happen.

I was taken to the offices of the Exploited and Missing Children's Unit of the Wichita Police Department in downtown Wichita. The two uniformed officers walked me into the building (which looked nothing like a police station) and down a hall, and down an elevator, and down another hall until I was forcefully sat down in an interrogation[21] room to be questioned by whoever would be doing the questioning. I was told to sit and wait. Just sit. I couldn't stand either because they'd taken an additional pair of cuffs and literally cuffed me to the floor. So, all I could do was sit.

---

18   Seriously, I also gave the parking lot a quick glance because I would not have been surprised to see Chris Hansen and his film crew coming around a corner somewhere.

19   I was later told that she would have had to be there to identify me, but I'm not sure if even that is accurate.

20   No leg room. Zero.

21   Either *Law & Order* is full of crap, or the Wichita Police Department had a very low budget, because there were no cameras, no giant windows with the two-way mirror or anything like that. It was just a room and a table and chairs. I hate to admit it, but it was quite anticlimactic.

This was the beginning.

Welcome to Hell

"Abandon All Hope, Ye Who Enter Here," reads the gate of Hell according to Canto III of Dante Alighieri's *Inferno*, the first work of *The Divine Comedy* but most commonly known as *Dante's Inferno*. I just knew, sitting at that table, the gates of Hell were directly before me, and, much like Dante, I anticipated an escort to show me through.[22] In the epic poem, Dante is accompanied by the classical poet Virgil, who tells him of all the fates and punishments of all the sinners who have been condemned to Hell. So, as I sat there, I was merely awaiting the arrival of my own Virgil to begin my journey through Hell as well.

After about an hour (or more)[23] of sitting in feverish contemplation, the door finally opened, and a detective walked in and sat down. He was extremely friendly and chipper and up-beat, which also seemed out-of-place. He had brownish-grayish hair in a buzz-cut hair style, much like a military cut, and his attire very much gave him that "cop" look, like on Law & Order or CSI.[24]

This man would be the Virgil for my journey into Hell, at least, for this one evening.

I agreed to talk to him, not because I wanted to talk to him, but because I wanted to know what he knew. I knew how to act, what to say (and more importantly, what *not* to say), so I wasn't afraid to engage him in a conversation with the goal of seeing what information he had. I didn't want to say or do anything because I was operating on insufficient information. And, I knew the best way to get information out of him was to allow him to accuse me of something. I knew why I

---

22 This imagery may seem a bit overly-dramatic (which perhaps it is), but it adequately conveys my mindset at the moment I sat in that interrogation room. I literally thought I was about to enter Hell. But that wouldn't happen until seven months later.

23 It felt like days.

24 This was neither good nor bad, just simply – was. He really had that police detective look. Granted, maybe I just remember it this way because, in this context, he was the good guy and I was the bad guy, but I just remember thinking that he had that "look."

was there and what I'd done, but what I did not know was what (or how much) he knew. Thus, my strategy for the entirety of the conversation was to simply deny everything, no matter what, and let the lawyers sort it out later.[25] So when he saw that I was open to discussing the situation, he slithered into the room and closed the door.

Interrogation

He pulled out the chair across the table from me, placed an iPad on the interrogation table, pressed a button, and began to speak.[26] "My name is Virgil. I'm a detective down here, alright, and, uh, this is, you know, my, my case going on, and stuff like that, and so basically you're here because of my investigation and stuff that, you know, I've been told and that I've been able to find out from my investigation, okay?"[27] He paused, I think expecting me to say something, but I just looked at him. I was still somewhat in shock. "I'm recording our conversation because, well, I don't take really good notes[28] and I don't want to have to ask you the same thing, you know, five, six, seven times and that kind of thing." He paused again. I said nothing. "Cool. Um, I got to tell it some stuff though because it is an audio recording so I'm going to tell it this is Detective Virgil,[29] the time is 19:46 hours

---

25 This would be my advice to anyone being interrogated for any crime. Deny it, let him book you, and let the lawyers sort it out later.

26 The following conversation is taken directly from the printed transcript of the recorded interview on the night of March 9, 2012, abridged, of course. The full transcript itself was twenty-seven pages long and much of it was just informational questioning without substance. But I have not altered the content or quotes, other than to correctly punctuate and format the narrative as well as altering identities for privacy purposes.

27 This is, word-for-word, what he said. I don't think he was nearly as nervous as I was (actually, I doubt he was nervous at all), but this was a situation where I was in a hurry to get to the point and he was taking his time. In retrospect, it was likely part of his strategy to break me down.

28 It also helped with the recreation of this scene for my book, so that was convenient.

29 I gave him this name to keep with the whole Dante's *Inferno* motif. Also with all the rather unflattering things I say about him, a moniker was necessary here. And while I am fully aware that the things I write seem mean-spirited, it illustrates my frame of mind at the time (because, from what I've heard, this detective is actually a really good person).

of March 9, 2012." I gave him a weird look, and he saw me grimace at him. He was telling me that he had to tell a small machine these things, as though the machine was going to get upset if it wasn't let in on the conversation and he didn't want to hurt its feelings. "This is regarding case number 12C013869. In the room with me, Kurt can you tell me your name?"

"Kurt Brundage," I replied like I was mocking his question;[30] he'd just told me my name, then asked me what my name was, which I can understand for the purposes of the recording, but it was still awkward, considering it was also a face-to-face conversation. Then he asked me endless questions about how to spell my name, my middle name, my address, etc.

He asked me if I lived in Lawrence, Kansas.

"Yes," I replied mechanically.

"Okay," he said. "That's a nice town. My wife and I enjoy going up there to visit."

I gave him a look that hopefully conveyed what I was thinking, which was, *Why are you telling me this? Don't try to be my friend.* I had no reason to be so rude to him, but I was, and I shouldn't have been. I think I was just in the initial stages of buckling under the pressure and this was my go-to response.

His questions continued: phone number, previous addresses, place of birth, social security number, race, height, weight, hair color, eye color, tattoos, etc.

Next, he started asking about family background: my wife's name, my mother, my father, where did they all live, what were their phone numbers,[31] etc. It all got quite tedious, and I was anxious to get to the

---

But for literary purposes, it illustrates the drastic change within me as a person from the beginning of this book (and frame of time) to the end.

30 Honestly, I really do regret being so rude, dismissive, and snarky to the guy. I mean, he was just doing his job, and in this situation, he was the good guy and I was the bad guy, plain and simple.

31 I didn't know anyone's phone number, and this would later prove to be a problem.

substance of the conversation; it was like watching crappy coming attractions before a movie that you didn't want to see in the first place.

"And, you work for Eudora High School. And, you're an English teacher," he said, as though he was letting me know something of which I wasn't immediately aware. "I noticed that you were an English teacher, uh, while you were here in Wichita too. Is that just your preference or is that just where they seem to stick ya or...?"

"That's what my degree is in," I said.

"That's what your degree is in," he said in a monotone voice of comprehension. "So you've been at Eudora for—"

"A year," I said, trying to finish his sentence and hurry the process along. "This is my first year," I reiterated, feeling this statement needed further clarification.

"Okay," he said, "so about eight months so far?"

So far? I thought to myself. The reality was, I would never be allowed back there again, and at that moment, I knew it. "Yeah," I replied with a somewhat empty glare.

"And," he said, beginning to speed things along a little, "you worked for East High for how long?"

"Five years," I replied.

"Uh, so, you've got — do you have a Bachelor's Degree or an advanced degree?" he asked.

"I have a Master's Degree," I replied with an elitist tone.[32]

"Master's Degree," he said in a voice that made it sound like the idea of a post-graduate degree was an alien concept to him. "In English?"

"No," I replied. "In education."

---

[32] I do certainly realize and understand how completely arrogant I was acting here. But it wasn't because I was being a tool. It was by design. I knew I needed to lay groundwork before the actual "interrogation" began that told him that he wasn't going to simply walk all over me.

"In education," he said, again repeating my previous sentence. That was really beginning to get frustrating.[33]

"Administration,"[34] I said, again feeling that I needed to clarify things for him.

"Where did you get your degree?" he asked.

"Wichita State," I replied.

"Have a religious preference?"

"Christian."

"Any particular faith?"

"Non-denominational," I said, hoping this would answer his question; it wasn't quite clear, but he got the gist.

The conversation was starting to drag. He asked more diagnostic informational questions about me which really didn't seem to matter but continued until I was asked about my cell phone and computer. Both had been in my car when I was arrested and were now in police custody.

"Cool," he said with a seemingly-impatient breath. "Alrighty." He paused. "Um, because this is an ongoing thing, I, I do have your phone and I do have your computer, you know, in a safe spot right now. I would like to have your permission because I know you've been talking to at least, you know, one person, uh, who's been, you know, visiting with the police department, uh, I would like to have your permission, you know, to just download, you know, the phone. Uh, call logs and text messages and that kind of stuff just to corroborate,[35] uh, what's going on. Do you have a problem with that?"

---

33   Granted, most of my frustration was with myself, but it manifested in me being a complete jerk, which I really do regret.

34   The technical name of my degree was a Master of Education in School Leadership. But "administration" just seemed quicker and easier at the time.

35   For the record, "corroborate" was the biggest word he used all evening.

"Go ahead,"[36] I said dismissively. I knew I didn't have anything incriminating on my phone. He could search it all he wanted.

"Okay," he said, seeming surprised that I consented so quickly. "How about your computer? Do you mind if, uh, we have a tech look thorough your computer and make sure there's no illegal stuff on there like, you know, child porn and that stuff?"

"Yes," I said casually. "Yeah, go ahead, there's nothing there." I shook my head, letting him know he'd be wasting his time.[37]

Evidently his iPad would feel left out if I didn't do something with that too, so he slid it over to me.

"Okay," he began, needing me to sign the release. "Um, what I need for you to do is kind of just read that over, you can read it to yourself or read it out loud if you'd like. Yeah, uh, and I will pull up the signature block for you here." Then he hit a wrong button and got confused and flustered.[38] "No, that's not what I wanted it to do. Go away." He was now talking to the iPad again. "That's what I wanted to do," he said with satisfaction. "When you get done," he began again, apparently talking to me again now, "I'll just have you sign right there and that way we can get started on that and maybe you won't have to be without that stuff for very long, okay?[39] I'm just using this one document for both your iPhone and your, uh, Gateway computer."

Then the conversation turned to substance abuse.

"Have you had any alcohol to drink in the last twenty-four hours?"

"No."

"Any prescription drugs in the last twenty-four hours?

"No."

---

36   At the moment, I remember thinking that I sounded like Edward Norton in American History X when he said "Go ahead..." when the principal threatened to expel him. It's weird what the mind does when it feels helpless and pressured at the same time. Mine makes movie references. Go figure.

37   There wasn't even any adult porn on my computer, let alone child porn.

38   Technology was not his forte.

39   This was a lie. They kept my phone and computer for weeks, even though there was nothing illegal on either of them.

"Any illegal drugs in the last twenty-four hours?"

"No."

"Have you had a head injury in the last twenty-four hours?"[40]

"No."

"Do you speak English?"

"I do," I said with as much sarcasm as I could muster.

"Yeah, you got a Master's Degree in it." He paused. "Or, a Master's Degree in — anyway and teach English." And at that point he had me read my Miranda Rights out loud. It kind of took away from my quintessential *Law & Order* moment when Lenny Brisco "reads me my rights" because I had to mindlessly read them from the screen of the iPad. I couldn't even get them read *to* me.[41]

When that was done he seemed finished with me, which didn't make any sense to me because, as near as I could tell, we hadn't even gotten started. "So," he said, standing up from his chair, "if you need anything, you know, kind of holler out a little bit and, you still good? You need a bottle of water or anything?"

"May I make a phone call?" I asked. Seemed like a legitimate question, or at least it was in the movies.[42]

"No."

"I need to at least let my wife know where I am," I said. Again, it seemed reasonable.

"Yeah, no," he said, which was the first time he'd really seemed rude, which again caught me off guard because he'd been so friendly until that point.

"No, I'm fine," I said, and he left.

---

40   I didn't expect this question. Seemed out of place. I mean, it makes sense, but it kind of caught me off guard at the time, though I tried to keep my responses as mechanical as possible.

41   This minor difference had a significant impact, however. At that moment, the experience went from being surreal (like I was watching myself in a movie about me) to being quite real (as I actually sat there in that actual situation).

42   Not being allowed to make a phone call made me feel more isolated from the world than I'd ever felt in my entire life. It changed from being escorted through Hell to falling aimlessly down the Rabbit Hole.

At this point, I was completely confused. Apparently, he didn't get the message that I was ready to have a conversation. So as he was making his way out the door, I told him I wanted to open up a dialogue.

I was ready to talk.

CHAPTER THREE

When Detective Virgil re-entered the interrogation room, he closed the door gently behind him. He sat down and pressed a button on his iPad. "Uh," he began, as he seemed to do often, "it's 20:15 hours." He paused. "Okay, so it's 20:15 hours and Kurt, uh, I, I, just, I'm putting this on here so that, you know, an attorney later can't say, uh, you know, held my client down and you twisted his arm and made him talk to you and that kind of stuff." The sheer quantity of times he used the word *stuff* was beginning to annoy me as well. "I was about to leave and you said you wanted to talk. Is that correct?"

"That's fine," I said. "Yes."

Face-off

"Okay," he said, adjusting his posture in his squeaky old metal chair across the table from me. He had this way of leaning his elbows on the table when he talked that seemed like he wanted to appear condescending. "Uh," he began, "so, yeah, I'm just trying to make sure that you know somewhere along the line they don't say, you know, oh, you twisted Kurt's arm so, that's not at all, right?"

"Correct," I said, unsure if he was talking to me or the iPad, but a response seemed pertinent.

"And you understand that you still have the right to an attorney and all that stuff that you initialed and you originally marked *No*."

"Yes." I said. "Right."

"Okay," he said. "Um, okay." He paused again. "Well what this is about is, I've been talking to some people. I've had this case for a while. I've been, kind of, you know, checking up on you and that kind of stuff. Uh, you know, I, I, know some things The, uh, young lady who you've been talking to on the phone, uh, you know, asked you to come down to Wichita. What's her name?"

"Taissa," I said.

"Taissa, okay," he said, sounding like I reminded him of her name. "Uh, Taissa is the only one that I could work out a believable situation, uh, you know, it's, it's been two, you know, it's close to the two year anniversary, um, you know, she graduated from high school and she's entering college and, you know, so all those things that would cause, you know, a young lady to think back and say, you know, what the heck, you know, it, it, it was working with her." He was just blabbering at this point. "The other young ladies and ladies I've been talking with, uh, you know, I, I couldn't—"

"I don't understand *all*," I said, confused, "*other*, I don't know who it—" I couldn't figure out if he was hinting at all the affairs I'd had at the school with other teachers, or if he thought I was having multiple relationships with multiple students. Regardless, I did not anticipate that particular question and it sort of threw me off-balance.[43]

"Okay," he said, "uh, I know of at least one other person, uh, at East High that things weren't exactly the way they ought to have been."

"I—" I said, mentally discombobulated for a moment, which is where I did not want to be. "Who?" Then it occurred to me that it was a ploy. *He didn't know of anyone else.* He was just seeing if there was,

---

simply by saying there *was* one, thinking I would throw someone's name out there — but there was no name to throw out there; a notion that was soon confirmed by his subsequent statement.[44]

"That's what I'm asking you," he said with a poker face. "I've, I've got the name and if, and when you tell me, I can say yep that's who I'm talking about."[45]

"I'm…" I began, not quite knowing how I was going to finish the sentence and trying to figure out how he was trying to lead me toward an additional confession for something that never happened.

"Okay," he said, cutting me off and forcefully pressing-on. "Uh, but, you know, mostly on, on Taissa, you know, I was able to, she came in and talked, talked to me about some stuff, and, you know, told me about some stuff." He was kind of stumbling over his thoughts since his ploy didn't work.

That was the moment when I could clearly see he was fishing for something that wasn't there, and *he* realized it, so he quickly swung the discussion back toward Taissa. This disappointed me a little, because the opportunity to prove him wrong was quite appealing. But seeing as how I was clearly not in the driver's seat of this discussion, I just went with the flow.

"I was parked," he went on, "you know, I was there when she called you here a couple of days ago and, you know, when she talked to you and it was closer to five minutes before you showed up at the restaurant, even though you said ten minutes, uh, and that kind of thing."

He rambled on for another minute or so, and I sort of tuned him out. There was a huge conflict going on within me. Half of my emotional-self was plagued with the guilt of what I'd done.[46] I knew I was caught, and I knew there was no way out, but that wasn't what

---

44   Finally, all those hours of watching *Law & Order* and *NCIS* paid-off.

45   This statement confirmed my theory.

46   And I am still plagued. Every. Single. Day.

hurt. What hurt was this: With every passing moment, it became more and more real. In my reality, it was real to me, it was real to Taissa, and it was real to my wife. Otherwise, it didn't exist. But now, sitting in an interrogation room with a detective, it was suddenly *very* real. And the harshness of this new reality compounded the guilt of what I'd done. The other half of my emotional-self was the cocky, arrogant, strategic, calculating, and intellectual person — my *Good Will Hunting* half, as I call it — as I tried to out-strategize the detective by giving him just enough information for him to give me the information I was seeking. It was a chess match to me, and I was trying to think ten moves ahead of him; it was a poker game, and I was obviously bluffing.

"...Taissa," he said in a sentence I wasn't listening to; her name caught my attention. "Explain to me the situation with Taissa."

"Taissa and I," I said, knowing this was my first move of the chess game, "became real close after she told me about something that happened with her and some guy and we just became friends. She — when she wasn't a student anymore she, we just became friends and, um, it was just because she would come to my classroom about every day and I just kind of forged a real strong — or at least what I considered kind of a strong — friendship that, uh, apparently didn't work out." This statement obviously didn't come out as well as I'd hoped. My emotional and intellectual selves were at war with one another, and my ability to vocally relay an idea was the first casualty.[47]

"Okay," he said inquisitively. "What do you mean by 'apparently didn't work out'?"

Ugh, I thought to myself. *Now I have to explain the B.S. I just fed him.*[48] This conversation was not going well for me.

---

47   As I waged this internal battle with myself, it only made me feel like more of a crappy human being. I was at a point in my life when I was trying to outsmart a cop in an interrogation room. Clearly, my life had not gone as planned – I'd ruined it, and I couldn't even find the pieces to put it back together.

48   I was hoping this wouldn't happen.

"I don't know," I said, truthfully. I really didn't know. I'd reached the desperate point of just making it all up as I went along.[49] If I'd had a game plan (which I thought I did), it was ditched, and I was at the *winging-it* point. "I'm still trying to arrange all these thoughts in my head[50] because I'm trying to figure out what—" I stopped mid-sentence.[51] This was actually quite an honest statement, though not in the context I think he perceived it. I think he thought I was just confused about the situation, but in reality, I was confused about what to say and what wording to use — what information to give him. I thought I was crystal-clear on the situation; I was just struggling to control the information I wanted him to have.

"Okay," he said.[52] "When — when was this friendship that you forged with Taissa?" It annoyed me that he used the word *forged*, simply because I used it. So, I felt like he was subtly mocking me. "When about was that?" he asked.

"This would have been about—" I thought for a second, choosing my words wisely, but then it occurred to me that he was asking me questions to which he already knew the answer, so these inquiries were more for corroboration and/or confirmation of her story, which was fine. Facts were facts. "...about two years ago."

"Okay," he said (again). "About what month was that?"

"Goodness," I said with a sigh. He wanted details. I knew the details — all of them — but I wasn't going to give him any more

---

49   Not making up facts, but rather, making up how I was going to keep the conversation going without confessing anything.

50   True statement.

51   If there's one thing I did well, it would be my restraint from just spilling everything. All the guilt was heavy and I wanted to just tell him (or anyone) exactly what happened because all the secrecy was like carrying a ton of bricks, and I just wanted to put them all down. But, so far, I'd kept it together well and played it close enough to the vest.

52   I think this was the point when he was starting to get frustrated with me, if he wasn't already.

than the absolute minimum.[53] "I don't know, I just remember it was basketball season, if that helps." That gave him a three or four-month window. He could fill in the blanks.

"Basketball season," he said, repeating my words. "Okay," he said, yet again. "Do you remember if it was first semester or second semester?"

"I don't remember," I said.[54]

"Okay," he chimed. "So if I told you January 2010, that would be about right?"

"I—" I began, pausing, knowing that it wasn't *about right*, that was *exactly right*, "take your word for it," which seemed like an appeasing and placating answer. "Yeah."

And on he went, asking me questions about the situation — questions to which he already knew the answer, none of which I strongly confirmed, but I never really denied anything either. He asked me if I knew how old she was, and I placated him. He asked me about the times we met outside of school, and I placated him. There was no point in denying anything that wasn't incriminating.

And then he brought up things which *were* incriminating. And this was when my *deny everything and let the lawyers sort it out* policy went into effect. He began asking me about the Saturday when we made-out in my truck in a parking lot, our very last physical exchange. It was only a matter of time before he circled around to this, so I had to face the music and field these difficult and humiliating questions.

---

53   Yes, facts were facts, but I did not want him to think I knew as many details as I actually did because I did not want him to press me for more information. The purpose of the conversation (for me) was to see what he knew, not tell him what I knew.

54   A complete lie. It was the first week of January. Second semester. But he didn't need to know that I remembered it with that much detail. My thinking was, if he didn't think I remembered very well, he wouldn't dig very deep because he'd eventually figure out that he wouldn't get anywhere; whereas, if I displayed to him that I remembered the details, then details would be exactly what he sought. No thank you.

Tough Questions

"Okay," he said. "Okay," he said again, apparently revving up for something. I was about to find out what. "So, how'd your fingers end up in her vagina?" His words were heavy and accusatory.

"Um, no!" I said.[55] *Deny everything and let the lawyers sort it out later.*

"How'd her hand end up on, your," he stumbled his words, "end up on your penis?"

"No." I said,[56] gathering my thoughts for his oncoming barrage of buzz-word questions. I think he was hoping words like "penis" and "vagina" would throw me off-balance. And to be honest, the first time they kind of did. But I saw it for what it was and kept my guard up. *Deny everything and let the lawyers sort it out later.*

"Okay dude," he said,[57] leaning back in his chair, crossing his leg over his knee, "here's the deal." He gave his forehead a rub, as though I was annoying him to the point of head pain. I think he honestly thought I was going to admit to everything, so there was a certain amount of defeat in his demeanor. "The phone call she made just a couple of days ago, alright, that I recorded, where she says she said something along the lines of I don't understand how a teacher that I'm supposed to trust could touch me like that, oh I'm sorry, it's all my fault, or something along those lines."

"Yes, I felt — I carry a lot of guilt," I muttered. *Wait, what did I just say?* Just when I thought I'd gotten a firm grasp on the situation — just when I thought my intellectual self was in control, my emotional self says something like this. This was my first and biggest mistake of the interrogation. I made two mistakes with this: First, I gave a solid affirmative statement by saying "Yes," and second, I gave him

---

55   I'm not entirely sure that this denial was a lie. You'd think this would be something I would specifically remember, and while I'm not completely certain, I'm pretty sure this didn't happen – though it nearly did.

56   A lie. This actually happened once.

57   Yes, he called me "dude."

insight into my emotional state,[58] which he could easily use to direct the interrogation. So, I had to find a way to verbally walk backwards through my own footprints in the snow.

"Uh hum," he said, nodding his head. He seemed to be avoiding eye-contact with me, which I thought was a little odd. But then again, nothing about this situation seemed normal.

"By allowing myself," I continued, "to become something more than just a mentor—" Honestly, I had no idea where I was going with this.

"Uh hum," he said again, still nodding.

"But, and," I said. Now I was the one stumbling over words. "Like, I held her sometimes." I had to give him something that might be perceived as "over-the-line" for a teacher without breaking the law. This seemed reasonable.[59]

"Uh hum," he said again. He was just letting me talk now, hoping I'd just start pouring my heart out.

"She would cry," I began, trying to restructure my strategy, "she'd cry on my shoulder a lot of times and I felt like that was—"

"Why?" he asked, interrupting me, which I found odd.

And then I paused. I stopped. I was tired, the guilt was heavy, and my intellectual self was just ready to say *I give up*, so I just leaned back with my I-don't-care demeanor. "You're not going to believe anything I say, are you?"[60]

"It's not that I don't believe what you're saying," he said, sounding like he was trying to take control of the discussion again, "it's that I *do* believe everything she's saying." This was just cop interrogation double-talk and I saw it for what it was, and I wasn't about to let him con me into saying anything I didn't want him to know. This statement revamped my intellectual-self and I was able to regain a little footing.

---

58   Because the truth is, I did (and still do) carry an immense amount of guilt over what I've done.

59   Obviously, the definition of "reasonable" at this particular juncture was quite relative.

60   Probably the most factual statement of the night.

"I understand," I said, trying to give him a defeatist tone. "I understand."

He started rambling on about the whole "she has no reason to lie" routine and I put on the appeasement act again and let him do the talking, but this time, I kept my affirmative answers in my pocket. All he knew was that I was listening to him, which, in and of itself, wasn't even completely true. I just kept giving him neutral statements such as, "I understand your point."

"Okay," he said, shifting his weight in his chair and changing the subject. "Um, you know the one, uh, legal, I guess, uh, for lack of, you know, better descriptor, uh, legal sexual contact you had at East High School…"

Freeze. This statement *really* threw me because he said *the one* instance. This moment told me he was not operating on (even close to) complete information. So, the only thought I had was, *Which one of the numerous teachers I slept with did he know about?* I was suddenly quite interested in the conversation.

"…was with Brittany, right?"

"I never had—" I said, stopping mid-sentence. It took me a minute to figure out what exactly he was talking about. Then I remembered. "Brittany was…" but I had no way at that moment to adequately finish the sentence. However, what I did do was give him a very discombobulated facial expression that he clearly misinterpreted; lucky for me.

"Oh, she's nuts," he said with a sardonic snicker.

Brittany was a woman who worked for a non-district organization that served, among others, high school students, and one of her "clients" was a student at East. I met her by happenstance in the school office one day, and she came back to my classroom to hang out. Over the next few weeks, we had a fling. I never had sex with her, but we made out a few times and she ended up being absolutely, completely, and utterly insane. Seriously, she *was* crazy. And apparently, Detective Virgil was fully aware of her thorough mental instability. To make a long story short, I had to file a Protection from Stalking order against her because not only did she stalk me at school, she stalked me at my home as well.[61] And since this was enacted at the school and the Wichita police officer assigned to East High School was aware of this, he told Detective Virgil during the investigation.

Judging by the detective's prompt "she's nuts" statement, he'd obviously spoken to her.

Of course, I wasn't about to even admit to that, so, of course, *deny everything and let the lawyers sort it out later.*

"She came on to me over and over again," I said with as much faux-denial as I could muster, "and I pushed her off numerous times." I paused. "I told other teachers about this."[62]

"Uh hum," he said. I couldn't tell if he believed me or not, but at this point, I didn't particularly care.

"There was never any 'legal sexual contact' because there was no sexual contact," I said.[63]

"Okay," he said, matter-of-factly, then started rambling again. He went on a rant about how Taissa waited to say anything about our relationship until she was out of school because she was scared of rumors, as though I was going to start bad rumors about her (or something), which struck me as complete ridiculousness, but I'd given-up trying to figure out her motives. And by now, her motives didn't matter — *I was the one at fault, and I knew it.* The situation was obvious, so the "why" questions were moot. I'd reached the point in the process when I just wanted to know what was going to happen next. Having received all the information out of the detective that I wanted (or thought I would get), I just wanted to know what the charges were.

61　She actually violated this order by coming to the school and driving by my car in the parking lot; I promptly had her arrested.

62　This statement was true. I did tell the teachers around me my (sanitized) side of the story.

63　Total lie. But I was getting tired and I didn't care anymore.

"So, there's three counts of rape?" I asked.

"Three counts of rape, a count of attempted rape, two counts of aggravated indecent liberties." He gave me a look that told me he was trying to gauge my reaction to this statement.

"I don't understand where this is coming from, but—" I stopped talking. The charges genuinely made no sense to me. There were more charges against me than there were physical interactions that I'd actually had with Taissa. I was obviously being over-charged, but arguing this point would have been imprudent. "It seems, just, like a laundry list of things[64] for no longer than, um, I knew her." I kind of wanted it on record, without admitting anything, that the mere quantity of charges was illogical. But other than that, I just let it go. Nothing was going to change while I sat in that little room, chained to that little table.

That was the juncture when I just shut-down. I was done. He kept asking questions, and I just kept saying "No."

After asking me the same questions repeatedly for the next few minutes, he changed strategies and made one last-ditch effort to con me into admitting to something.

"What I've got," he began in yet another diatribe, "is, you know, I've got either, you know, a series of, you know, silly lustful mistakes, or, you know, you're a predator, you know and you're, you're, you're fishing in an aquarium, alright, you're fishing in an aquarium being the high school and, and you're a sexual predator, or you found a girl you thought was cute and you made some silly mistakes, which is, why, you know; which is it? Are you a predator or did you make some silly mistakes?"

He was trying to get me caught between an either/or statement, but I immediately saw right through it. His strategy was that I would

---

64   This kind of over-charging is common practice in cases like this. Charges stemming from the original arrest are always trumped-up because they make for better media coverage and when the prosecutor actually files the charges in court, it appears that he's doing the person a favor by not filing all the original charges, and therefore doesn't have to give up as much ground when it comes time to plea-bargain.

immediately deny being a "sexual predator" and take the "silly mistake" option, because "silly mistake" isn't nearly as bad as "sexual predator;" but either way, it would result in me admitting to what happened. And I certainly wasn't about to do this. So for the next few minutes, I simply found as many ways to side-step the question as I could conjure.

But the simple fact is, I was absolutely guilty. I knew it and he knew it. At the heart of the interrogation, whether or not I'd done it was never really the issue; the issue was whether or not he could find a way for me to say, in some way, shape, or form, *I did it*. And that was not happening. So, after a few more minutes of my denials, he finally grew impatient, stood up, and walked to the door.

"Alright," he said, pretending to stop the recorder on the iPad, but I could see that it was still recording, "if you decide you want to tell me what's actually going on, I'll be, uh, taking care of some paper work and, uh, just holler at me.

"Well, I mean—" I said

"Well," he said, interrupting me, "are you going to keep trying to, you know, blow smoke up my rear?"

"No."

"Or are you actually going to tell me what's going on, dude?"[65]

"I'm just—"

"Because," he said, interrupting me again, "I'm not going to sit here and just have you blowing smoke. If you want to tell me what's going on, I'm, I'm willing to sit here and listen."[66]

"I'm trying to—"

"But you're either a predator," he said, interrupting me yet again, "or you made a silly mistake because I know that things happened." When he said this, it occurred to me that he was clearly out of ideas,

---

65   He kept using the word "dude" and it was getting weird.

66   Translation: "Let me know when you're ready to confess."

out of strategies, and he was giving up; he was just recycling his ploys now. So, it was time for me to end the discussion.

That was about as much of this conversation as I could take. This guy was getting irritated because I wouldn't just readily admit to what I'd done. He stopped the iPad's recording function and began to leave the room.

"You know what, man," I said, leaning back in my chair and crossing my arms in as much of a defiant manner as I could muster, "I'm done talking. Just process me."[67]

"Okay," he said, not seeming like he cared, and he left the room.

I sat for a few more minutes (or perhaps an hour, or more) and replayed the interrogation in my head. I pretty much knew I was screwed. The reality of the situation was getting heavier and heavier, and all I could see in my mind's eye was the vision of my wife and daughter, and how I was convinced, at that moment, I would never see either of them again. And I knew I deserved it. I deserved all of it. I kept thinking to myself that my marriage and my family were blessings of which I was no longer worthy. The self-loathing began, and it would not stop any time soon.[68]

Eventually, the same two uniformed cops who brought me to this incognito building reentered the room, unhooked my foot from the table, and cuffed my hands back behind my back. We made our way to the elevator and back out the front door, into the police car, down the street a few miles, up to a building, down a ramp, through some very large retracting doors, and into the Sedgwick County Jail where I would spend the next seventeen hours.

---

67   Admittedly, at this point, I was mentally and emotionally exhausted.

68   In fact, it would last for *years*…

CHAPTER FOUR

One cliché I never really understood until that moment was, "It just got real." I mean, I essentially understood it in a comedic context (which was where I'd typically encountered this particular quip), but I never understood how something could get "real" until I took my first steps into the Sedgwick County Jail. And the one thing that made it "real" was the smell. Granted, it was real when I felt the handcuffs on my wrists, and it was real when Detective Virgil was interrogating me, but it never really felt real until I was escorted in that first door and the stench of jail invaded my nostrils.

There's an episode in Season Seven of *House M.D.* where Dr. House sends his doctors to break into someone's house to look for clues about a patient's illness, and they are busted by the police and arrested. After finally being released, Dr. Taub, one of House's doctors, remarked in a depressingly-comedic tone, "I smell like jail." But as comical and whimsical as that line sounded on television, I happen to know for a (very serious) fact that such a smell *does* exist. And it's putrid.

The moment I smelled the foul air of the Sedgwick County Jail, it all suddenly became *real*.

Seventeen Hours

The worst span of time of my entire life.[69] Getting there was a crystal-clear blur and only two constant thoughts were racing through my mind: "I will never see my wife and daughter again," and "How can I most efficiently and painlessly end my life?" The line that kept repeating in my mind was another line from *House M.D.*: "Pills are the simplest." And with every flash into my memory of my daughter's smiling face — and how I thought I would never see her again, or hug her, or hear her laugh; or kiss my wife, or see her beautiful smile — all I could do was fantasize on how I was going to end my own life. Living, as far as I was concerned, was no longer an option.

It was the middle of the night. As I lay on the rock-solid jailhouse cot in the Sedgwick County Jail, surrounded by eight or nine other cots filled with snoring inmates or absurd and mindless conversations, I pretended to sleep. The air was heavy, leaving an odd aftertaste in my uncomfortably-dry mouth. The jail smelled awful, like a musty old warehouse populated with homeless squatters and drug addicts; it smelled like misery and hopelessness — it smelled like shame. The jail's soundtrack was that of a muffled riot zone with the occasional bangs, slams, and shouts of the profanity-ridden manifestos and diatribes of the imprisoned. This was what I imagined Hell to sound like after reading *Inferno*. However, to everyone around me (who appeared to have been there before), it was business-as-usual.

The walls, the ceiling, and the floors were all the same color — not white, but not tan. It was like a very-light taupe. "They say taupe is very soothing." And the only things differing from this motif were the trim around the multi-person cell windows (an uncomfortable shade of brownish-maroon); and the cots, (which were a dark faded metal grayish brown, varying in degrees of rust, with dirty dark-pale green mattresses with worn rips exposing the white*ish* interior padding). There were no bars — all the "cells" were brick rooms with windows (trimmed in brownish-maroon) which lined the perimeter of the

---

69   Well, at the time. That night would be trumped seven months later.

booking area of the jail. There was a seating area out in the open center of the booking area, populated by uncomfortably-dark blue chairs — a waiting area, but no one was waiting; a television, but no one was watching. Sporadically-placed large cylindrical pillars filled any fluid space in the empty waiting area, some holding a peculiar apparatus that anyone who hadn't been to jail would describe as a "payphone without a coin slot;" but to someone who had been (or was) in jail, it was a lifeline to the outside world.

Everyone was in "street clothes," the clothes they wore when arrested. No one at this stage of the jail process had been taken to the housing area yet or given their jail jumpsuits, and with the swiftness of the "processing" phase, it wouldn't be anytime soon. But occasionally, a trustee[70] wearing a brown jumpsuit with "SEDGWICK COUNTY JAIL" stenciled in large black lettering on the back would walk through. When I was booked into jail, I was wearing a long-sleeve white t-shirt under a dark blue short-sleeved t-shirt and a black jacket. As I curled on the cot (which had a mattress no more than four inches thick and was folded-down at the head to simulate a pillow, riddled with rips and tears, probably infested with numerous insects and parasites), I had taken my coat off and covered as much of my upper-body and head as I could. I had also taken off my long-sleeve shirt and was clutching it in my arms like a teddy bear. But I'd taken it off for a reason.

Death Wish

The decision was mine to die. I felt 20,000 leagues beneath life's rock-bottom and all I wanted was to end the pain that I was in; I wanted to prevent the pain that my family was going to experience once my crime was exposed by the media. I took a sleeve of the long-sleeve t-shirt in my clutches and stretched it out as far as I could under the dark cover of my jacket. I wrapped it around my neck, tucked one end inside the other, and pulled on both sides as hard as I

---

70   A "trustee" is the jail equivalent of a "teacher assistant."

could, tight around my jugular veins. I was ready to die, and this was how I was going to make it happen.

Why couldn't I have been given the same choice Kurt Russell was given in *Escape from New York* before they sent him to the island? I would have promptly said, "Yes, please."

I pulled — as hard as I could — on each end of the shirt, tightening it around my throat. I could feel my breathing constrict. I could feel my head swell. I could feel my pulse pounding helplessly in my neck, struggling to pump blood to my brain. I could feel myself slipping away, and I was ready. Nevertheless, some primal human instinct in me kept reaching up at the last second and loosening the strangling of my neck. Something was keeping me from completing the literal death I so desired, leaving me only with the figurative death which was already set into motion (and in some ways, was set in motion years earlier).

I tried — over and over again — to die. I have no idea how many times (or over how many hours) I attempted to tighten that shirt sleeve around my neck, trying desperately to leave this life. But an instinct unknown to myself kept driving me to reach up and loosen the grip of death around my neck at the last possible moment, just before losing consciousness.

I came extremely close once, feeling myself slipping away, hearing the world around me echo, as if I was suddenly inside a giant tin can, and all I saw was black. Had I not reached up to loosen the sleeve that time, I definitely would have slipped away. But there was something keeping me alive, something beyond me. This continued for hours, trying repeatedly, but never succeeding.

As those agonizing hours wore-on, my only recourse was to drown myself in my own cerebral wilderness. Sitting in jail isn't exactly a conversational environment, chatting with peers about the weather or sports or work or anything else mundane. And in fact, I was asked the question several times, "What are you in for?" I remember thinking to myself how cliché that was, and how I only thought people said that on hokey TV cop shows, but there were numerous people asking me that exact question. Logic then indicated, if one cliché is true, then the other about inmates beating the hell out of "guys like me" with "my crime" may not be fictitious. And if they found out I was a teacher, it would just make it all-the-worse.

At that moment, another option entered my head. *What if I told the other five or six guys in my cell what I was actually in for, and let them do what they wanted?* Hopefully, then, I wouldn't need a shirt-sleeve, just a few quality kicks to the head from some career criminal who couldn't care less whether or not he was incarcerated for the rest of his meaningless life.

So, a few minutes later, when the next person asked me why I was arrested, I prepared myself for the possible upcoming painful torture, and said, "Just some stuff from like two years ago."

"Oh, yeah, I know what that's like," he replied.

Wait, *what? Why didn't I say it?* Why didn't I just tell him that I'm in jail because I was a teacher who had a relationship with one of my former students? Why didn't those words enter the air with the tone of my voice? It's what I *meant* to say. It's what I'd *planned* to say, and when I inhaled to formulate those thoughts into words, some entirely different (and innocuous) words floated into the atmosphere. *What happened?*

I'd locked the door, and thrown away the key. There was someone in my head, but it wasn't me.

Booked

As I sat there on my cot, trying figure out where my words went wrong, a frumpy jail deputy with a callous expression on his face unlocked the cell door and stepped in, reading from a note card and never looking up.

"Brundage," he said, mechanically.

Without speaking, I stood up and walked toward him. He led me to an area just outside the door in front of a cheap digital camera.

I'd been in jail for what seemed like days, but was only about ten hours (so far), and I was just now about to be photographed and fingerprinted.[71]

"Stand there," he said, pointing to a worn-down mark on the floor in front of a bland grayish background. He never told me to look at the camera, and even if he had, I don't think I could have mustered the will to do so. I was at the lowest point of my entire life, and looking anywhere but down was beyond any feasible ability remaining in my broken body and mind. I knew this picture would eventually be on every television news station in Wichita and Kansas City,[72] and looking those inevitable viewers in the eye was something I was not prepared to do.

I don't remember the picture snapping, but the deputy simply muttered, "Okay, over here," and pointed to an elevated table where I would be fingerprinted.

Being fingerprinted was a mundane process as well; not in the literal sense, but in how the deputy gripped my hands and fingers one by one, rolled them through ink, and placed them on the fingerprint card.[73] I remember wondering what matter of conversation should take place at that point, based on society's social contract. Then it occurred to me that there really was no social contract — I was in a place with the sole purpose of removing me from society, so as far as social propriety was concerned, all bets were off. I elected to remain silent.

In the one instance I elected to break the silence, I asked, "What happens now?" The deputy responded, again without looking at me as he continued to roll my fingers onto the ink and fingerprint cards.

---

71   The booking process in the county jail is nowhere near as quick as TV makes it seem. Seriously, it was like seven to ten hours before they even began to process me. Then again, it's not exactly a customer service industry.

72   Since my crime was committed in Wichita, but I was teaching (at the time) at a school near the Kansas City area, both metro news cycles covered my story.

73   I thought this process was done with a little more technology, considering it was 2012, but I guess that's just one more area where Wichita is behind the rest of civilization.

"You'll go upstairs in a while. With your crime, you'll get your own cell."

With your crime...

I understood.

"What about bail?" I asked.

"You won't get bail. With what you're charged with, you'll be here until they get you in front of a judge on Monday morning." Again, he didn't even look at me.

From what I could tell, it was the early hours of Saturday, maybe 4AM; I was arrested Friday night. The thought of spending the weekend in jail was torturous, partly because I had nothing but my own assumptions to prepare me for what the experience might be like; but mostly, I would be away from my wife and daughter. But regardless, I just stood there, still numb from the shock of everything that had gone on. I only mustered the strength to pathetically reply, "Okay."

When he finished, he sat me in a waiting chair next to the mug shot camera and said, "Wait there." He walked off to a desk behind me and I waited, looking around, thinking to myself, *I deserve to be here, but I don't belong here. My life is over.*[74]

He came back and handed me a small card with a series of hastily-scribbled numbers.

"This is for your phone calls. Pick up a phone and enter that code."

I nodded in comprehension.

However, I had one significant problem: I knew no one's phone number. In the day and age of cell phones, there was no need to remember a phone number. Simply entering a person's phone number into my iPhone and saving the contact information under their name was the norm.[75] The only phone number in my memory was the phone number of my parents' house growing up. But of course, only

---

74   I specifically remember thinking this, and I still have no idea what it means.

75   Another casualty of the modern technology-driven society. Seriously, the only reason I know my wife's cell phone number now is from dialing it twice-a-day on a prison telephone.

a few weeks prior, they'd terminated that phone number and joined much of the rest of the world in only having cell phones themselves and no house phone. I didn't even know my wife's cell phone number. I was stuck.

He led me back to a holding cell — a different one this time — and I found a bed where I could again sulk in my own life's failures.

As I sat, minutes felt like hours, hours felt like days, and I was petrified to find out what days would feel like. All I could do was pray — and pray, I did. Praying gave me a sense of strength and peace, which may or may not have been from a god or God that may or may not exist, but it got me through the preceding hours. So still I sat, casting a melancholy gaze upon the linoleum tile floor, silently talking to God. I didn't expect an answer, I merely hoped He was listening. I convinced myself that this was happening for a reason beyond my understanding, other than my errant choices. The only thing providing any semblance of comfort (about anything) was the thought that I didn't know everything, or anything. And as I thought — and prayed — I still couldn't lift my eyes from the floor.

So, there I sat. Awake. Sleep in any way, shape, or form was no longer an option.[76] It was reaching early morning and I had no way of communicating with the outside world. The police had my cell phone — which they would keep as evidence[77] — so I had no one's phone number.

I'd given up on death; I'd given up on life. Life would be much more painful, and at that point, my mindset was that I simply deserved whatever was coming to me.

A Good Deed

As I waited, a young man — likely in his mid-twenties — was brought into my holding cell, and he was visibly distraught. He paced

---

76 Not that it ever was to start with.

77 Even though there was nothing on it.

the cell, worried, stressed, and uncomfortable. From the look of his familiar demeanor regarding the jail surroundings, I guessed that he'd been there (or somewhere similar) before. However, something else was bothering him. I'm not sure why, but I spoke to him.

"Are you okay, man? Need to talk?" I asked.

He was tall, fit, with short dark brown hair and sleeve tattoos, but did not seem at all intimidating. He sat down on an adjacent cot and began to speak.

"They brought me in and I shouldn't even be here!" he said hastily. "I can't believe what's happening. I'm so worried about my wife, bro. I can't believe this." His head hung between his shoulders as though he wore an anvil around his neck, and he slowly rocked back and forth rubbing his hands together.

"What happened?" I asked.

He began his story.

"We just came in town last night. It's our anniversary. We got a motel room by the highway and we were just hanging out, us two and my buddy and my wife's dog.[78] But it was getting late and we got into an argument and she was getting all emotional and so my buddy was just sitting there in the hotel room while we fought so he decided he'd get up and go outside. Well when he opened the door, my wife's dog ran out and took off. We chased it but it ran onto the off ramp of the highway next to the motel. And before I could do anything, this car just runs over it! I saw it, my wife saw it, it just ran over her dog! So she starts freaking out and runs out onto the highway and grabs the dog and brings it to the side of the road, and when I run up to get her off the highway, she starts crying and yelling and hitting me! She was freaking out, bro!"

He was getting more and more worked-up as he spoke.

---

78   I found this to be a very odd cast of characters in his story, considering it was a trip for his anniversary, but then again, by that point in the night (or morning, or whenever), nothing surprised me anymore, nothing seemed odd; everything just was.

"Then," he continued, "the cops drove up and asked us what was going on and I tried to tell them what was happening, but they just put us both in cuffs and put us in separate cars. I don't even know where my buddy went to, he was gone.[79] So the cops ran my name through the system and saw that I had a warrant. So they brought me to jail. And now I don't even know how my wife is doing! I'm scared, bro, she's so emotional!"

I felt sorry for them; I really did. I wanted to help. He and I talked for nearly an hour, and I did my best to try to convince him that everything was going to be okay, that his wife was okay, and that everything would work out.[80] I told him that the best thing he could do was stop replaying the scene in his mind, and just stay positive, that his wife would call, that he would be bailed out soon enough.

As we spoke, a deputy opened the holding cell door and pointed at him.

"Your wife called," the deputy said to him. "She's coming to pick up your stuff. She's seeing about your bail." He lifted his head from between his shoulders and seemed to breathe a sigh of relief, as he gave me what seemed to be a glance of thanks. And honestly, it really felt good to talk this guy through his difficulties, as though I was doing just a little bit of good for someone, even though I was *there* for doing so much evil.

The deputy then looked at me. "Brundage. Come here."

---

79   In retrospect, I can totally relate to him being upset about his best friend just disappearing when the situation got difficult.

80   I think I was trying to convince myself of this very same thing at the very same time. I was talking to him, but maybe I was talking to me too.

CHAPTER FIVE

stepped out of the holding cell and the jail deputy handed me a scrap of paper. "Your dad called. Here's the number," he said, and pointed to a phone on a nearby pillar. I approached the phone quickly and enthusiastically, as if I was calling to check if I had the winning lottery number. It took several attempts at navigating the touch-tone instructions, but as I dialed the numbers for my "inmate code" followed by the phone number on the torn piece of paper, I wasn't sure what I was going to say when my father answered.[81]

My Phone Call

All I knew was that I wanted to talk to someone from the outside world. I needed to know someone out there cared. I needed to know there was still a world outside of the walls around me. It felt like I'd been in jail for days.

"Hello," said a voice that I was so happy to hear, tears came to my eyes.[82] It was my wife.

"I'm so sorry," was all I could say.

---

81   I mean, seriously, how do you even begin a conversation like that?

82   No lie.

She knew why I was arrested, and knew ahead of time that, once I left her at my parents' house where we were visiting, that if I didn't send her a text message within thirty minutes, she would know that I'd been arrested.

"We're trying to get you out," she said with emotion and panic in her voice. I'd never heard her speak like that, and it hurt.

"They're not letting me out. The deputy said I'm not getting bail," I told her. Hearing her voice was Heaven at that particular moment.

"Yes you are. Your bail is $100,000.[83] Your dad has been on the phone with the jail, so we're seeing what we can do to get you bonded out."

"Have you called a bail bondsman yet?" I asked.

"No, we need to find the money first.[84] Should I call your mom?" She paused; so did I.

My first inclination when she asked me that was to say *No*. I knew this was going to break my mother's heart, and to ask her for money on top of that seemed like adding insult to injury, and I just couldn't do that to her.

She interrupted my thoughts.

"I want you out of jail. We need to call her."

I paused. "Okay," I replied reluctantly. I didn't have any fight left in me. "I'm so sorry," I said, choking back tears.

"It's okay," she said with determination. "We'll get through this."[85]

As I walked away from the phone and back to my holding cell, the first glimmer of hope lifted me a little. I hadn't slept all night and

---

83   Thus, someone would need to come up with $10,000 to pay a bail bondsman to get me out of jail; in this case, my parents somehow pooled together this money. Never question parents' dedication to their children. Ever.

84   For a middle-class family, pulling $10,000 out of thin air wasn't as easy as a trip to the ATM. From what my dad told me years later, it included the maxing-out of several credit cards, the emptying of checking and savings accounts, and convincing the bondsman to take monthly payments on the remaining balance they couldn't acquire.

85   This would not be the last time she spoke these words to me. In fact, she says it to me still.

I was wearing down — mentally and physically — but finding out I might be going home was maybe a tiny prayer answered.

But if I thought time was slow overnight, it stood still as I waited to hear back from them, or hear that I was allowed to leave.

As I waited, I was escorted to the jail nurse who conducted a verbal physical evaluation of me. She showered me with a barrage of questions which I answered mechanically, hoping I could simply tell her what she needed to hear so that I'd be allowed to go home, if-and-when I was able.

"Do you smoke?"

"No."

"Do you drink?"

"Rarely."

"Do you do any illegal drugs?"

"No."

"Had any suicidal thoughts?"

"No."

That was a lie.[86]

As the questions wore on, I kept looking back, hoping a deputy was looking for me, to tell me my wife was there to pick me up. And when the nurse finished, I slowly walked back to the outer holding area until I was instructed to return to my cell. I did. And I waited.

A deputy finally came into my cell and called my name. I stood up, gathered my things, and he looked at me like I was breaking a rule.

"You're next to go upstairs,"[87] he said. I remember feeling surprised that a deputy actually made eye-contact with me.

"What's upstairs?" I asked.

"Housing," he replied. He was no longer looking at me. He closed the door, locked it with an uncomfortable *thud,* and left. My heart made a similar sound.

---

86   Best lie I've ever told. I didn't know it at the time, but I am beyond glad I said "No."

87   Essentially, this meant I wasn't leaving the jail any time soon.

"You ain't been to jail before, have you?" I looked around to see if this question was intended for me. It was. It was the guy I'd been talking to about his wife and their dog.

"Nope," I said. I felt deflated.

"Housing is where you get your jumpsuit. Means you'll be here a while," he said, as if he were giving me details on how to operate a copy machine. I didn't take offense to his tone, however, because it became apparent at that moment that he'd been through this routine more than a few times.

Any hope that I'd had after talking to my wife was shattered. Apparently, someone knew something I didn't, and I was going to be stuck in jail; for how long, I didn't know.

An hour passed. Letting us sit and stew in these holding cells seemed to be the status quo. Their interest in getting inmates to their final destination in a quick and efficient manner didn't seem to be a high priority.

Freedom Again

When the door opened again, and my name was called, I stood up, ready to enter the next phase of the correctional system. The only thing I could think about was the initial scene in *The Shawshank Redemption* when Tim Robbins' character, Andy DuFresne was taken to prison for the first time. Although I was reasonably certain it wouldn't be like that, my scope of experience in this realm was relatively limited.

I walked toward the deputy at the door with my head hanging in disgrace.

"You're bonded out," he said to me, still mechanically and without emotion, though this was a different deputy than before. "Go to the desk for your things and your paperwork."

I didn't smile, I didn't grin, I didn't even quicken my step with the knowledge that I was going home. I stopped for a second, not looking up, and sighed the deepest sigh of my life. It was as if I was exhaling every demon of doubt and fear of that place which had burrowed within my soul, and all I knew was that I wanted to feel my wife's arms around me, and hear my six-year-old daughter say, "Hi Daddy!"

I walked to the desk and was presented with my personal items — keys, wallet, loose change — and was told to sign a piece of paper, and then another piece of paper, then I was told to wait.

Standing at the chest-high green(ish)-blue(ish)-puke(ish)-colored desk, waiting to be released, wasn't as bad as one would think, because I knew the next step was freedom.[88] However, as I stood there, I could hear the deputies around the corner behind the desk, including the one who had just processed me, making jokes amongst themselves about my charges.[89] They all stood in their matching light-blue shirts and dark-puke-blue pants[90] in a circle around the corner behind the copy machine, cackling and making jokes — at my expense.

"He was her teacher?" one of them remarked with a snicker. Another deputy chimed-in, "Here hottie, why don't you turn around and hike that skirt up and I'll give you today's lesson!"

They all laughed.[91]

I probably deserved it.

He returned and pointed to the door to my left and said, "Right out that way."

I approached the giant door and stopped. It slowly opened by remote, I stepped through to another door, the door behind me closed, the door in front of me opened, and I stepped out; I stepped out into the clear viewing of my wife, my father, and an enormous bearded man whom I assumed was the bail bond person. I walked over to my beautiful wife and she hugged me harder than I could ever have

---

88 Sort of. I haven't felt true freedom since the nanosecond before I was arrested.

89 Seriously. They did this. And I could hear all of it clearly; I think they knew this, and didn't care.

90 These were the same uniforms that the actual Sherriff's deputies wore, except I think these were the deputies they didn't trust with a gun; or a car for that matter.

91 I remember wondering how Taissa would have felt if they'd known they were joking about her like that, or how the general public would feel about the deputies joking about a sex crime victim like that. But they didn't seem to care either way.

hugged her. At that moment, I knew that seven years earlier, when she said, "For better or worse, till death do us part," *she meant it.*

I signed a paper for the bail bond guy, affixing my signature and dating it, March 10, 2012, promising I would appear for my subsequent court dates. My dad and wife shook his hand, thanking him for his help with the payment arrangements, and we all departed.

The day was sunny, clear, and spring-like. The air smelled clean and the sun was warm. Clearly, the thematic feel of the weather outside did not fit the looming storms of my life.

They drove us to get my wife's car, which I had been driving when I was arrested and was still sitting in the parking lot where I'd been taken into custody. We then went back to my father's house where we would be spending the weekend.

I was simply glad I could finally put an end to the worst and longest night of my life. For much of the rest of that day, I sat on my dad's porch, in silence, frozen.

"It was not guilt that froze me.
I had taught myself never to feel guilt.
It was not a ghastly sense of loss that froze me.
I had taught myself to covet nothing.
It was not a loathing of death that froze me.
I had taught myself to think of death as a friend.
It was not heartbroken rage against injustice that froze me.
I had taught myself that a human being might as well look for diamond tiaras in the gutter as for rewards and punishments that were fair.
It was not the thought that I was so unloved that froze me.
I had taught myself to do without love.
It was not the thought that God was cruel that froze me.
I had taught myself never to expect anything from Him.
What froze me was the fact that I had absolutely no reason to move in any direction."[92]

———————

92   From *Mother Night* by Kurt Vonnegut

The brief and lengthy journey had finally come to a merciful end. It was the longest night of my life — at that point. And I knew, without a doubt, the real journey was just beginning. It was only a matter of time before my face was on the news, my picture was in the paper, and my story was all over the Internet. I was about to become the media's latest sex scandal, and all I could do was hang my head in shame.

CHAPTER SIX

My family loves me, unconditionally. In fact, I don't think I ever truly understood the meaning of "unconditional love" until I was arrested. But from the moment my family pooled together $10,000 to post my bail the morning after my initial arrest, I began to understand what family is really all about. Family isn't just about a last name – family is a verb – family is a collective body.

That being said, if family is indeed a collective body, then I felt like the cancer that plagued that body. The reality of the situation was simple: My actions humiliated my family and caused them immeasurable pain. I offered them countless apologies and they accepted them countless times, but apologies don't change the past.

Death Wish 2.0

Not-so-suddenly (a long night in jail and $10,000 later), my name and mugshot were on the news and I was trying to forcibly exhale the lingering jailhouse stench from my nostrils. It all seemed so surreal, yet so painfully real. It was impossible to grasp the moment because the moment was indefinable. There was no one to blame but myself, nowhere to turn but inward, and nowhere to go but down. I'd been disgraced by my own actions and choices, and I'd disgraced my family, my friends, and my profession.

In my mind, I was through, and that's why, when we returned to Lawrence — on March 14, 2012 — I hastily swallowed an entire bottle of blood pressure medication, hoping my blackened heart would break, permanently.

My wife and daughter had just left our house. She was going up to the high school where I was no longer welcome (and was currently "on administrative leave, with pay") to clean out my belongings from my classroom. And when she left, I began to frantically pace our house, upstairs and downstairs, panicking, listening to the silence as it mocked me for ruining everything I'd ever worked for, ever wanted, ever dreamed of, and ever lost. My heart pounded and my thoughts raced. I couldn't bring myself to calm down. I wept uncontrollably, I breathed inconsistently, I mumbled incoherently.

So, in an act of depressive desperation, I went into our bathroom and opened the medicine cabinet. I found a bottle of blood pressure medication I'd been prescribed as an aid to my migraines. I'd barely taken any, so the bottle was more-or-less full. I walked down to the kitchen, opened a 2-liter bottle of 7-Up, poured the entire bottle of pills into my mouth, and began chugging from the bottle of soda. And after the last pill was swallowed and the last stinging gulp of carbonation had cleared my throat, I walked slowly to our bedroom. It felt like a long walk, like a condemned man being escorted to the gallows. I put on my most comfortable pair of Adidas basketball shorts and an oversized t-shirt, crawled into bed, and turned on the television.

I remember, trying to die.

I remember slowly slipping from consciousness, lying in bed watching *Seinfeld* reruns on TBS and trying to imagine that I was being mercifully put out of the misery of everyone around me — I believed my own misery to be well-deserved. During those long moments, as I felt myself slipping away (and my wife and daughter were in my classroom retrieving my belongings), a camera crew from Channel 6 News in Lawrence was setting up outside the school, preparing to do a story about me.

My public humiliation was just beginning.

But I'd given up. As I lay atop the comforter on our bed, I felt the darkness envelop me, like someone falling backwards into a midnight sea — in slow motion. And I swear I remember hearing the haunting chant of *Requiem Aeternam*, as heard during "Mercutio's Death" in the 1996 film version of *Romeo & Juliet*.

And then, nothing — nothingness — nothing.

My wife arrived home an hour or so later, and found me unresponsive. She did her best to wake me, but I did not regain consciousness. She yelled at me, splashed water on me, even slapped me and bit my finger. Finally, with no other options, she called 9-1-1.

"Daddy's sick," she said to our daughter as the paramedics carried my motionless body to the ambulance.

I was taken to the hospital in Lawrence where I remained in a coma for several days. On the second day, my wife was sitting at my bed side, watching as a ventilator breathed for me and the beep of my pulse monitor provided a slow and depressive rhythm to my life's swan song. But the silence was broken by the buzz of her phone — a text message from her sister.

"Please call me!! I know about Kurt, you can talk to me," read the text message from my wife's sister. Apparently, my wife's step-mother, who had always seemingly disliked me,[93] somehow found the story about me on a random small-town website before Wichita ever reported it. "Mom called me," said the subsequent text.

My wife replied, giving subtle details about why I was in the hospital.

"I love you and I'm here if you need to just talk. Keep me informed on how he is doing," her sister replied. "Is he stable or awake?"

---

93   We did manage to make amends after I was released from prison – well, sort of.

"He is in critical condition," my wife replied in her text. "He is on a ventilator and they are monitoring his heart and they have given him charcoal to help absorb the meds to flush them out."

"Okay," her sister replied, "You doing okay?"

"Yes," my wife texted. "Just sitting and waiting." In my mind's eye, I can still see her, sitting at my hospital bed, waiting for me to wake up.

Cuckoo's Nest

After finally waking, I was held at the hospital for a few more days for observation. The prescription overdose had the severe side-effect of temporary paralysis; I couldn't walk. Every time I had to use the bathroom (after they painfully removed the catheter), I had to have a nurse or my wife walk me to the bathroom, then walk me out. It was humiliating.

Upon being *medically* cleared, I was sent to a mental hospital in Topeka. Here's some context to adequately illustrate why this was particularly humiliating for me: My second job out of college (circa 2005) was working as a case manager for the county department of mental health. And part of my job was determining when one of my clients necessitated hospitalization for their mental health issues.

Then, there I sat, in their shoes.

I was not in the mental hospital by choice. I was taken from the ICU by way of "secure transport" to the asylum where I was admitted, given a room, and prodded with endless evaluations, counseling sessions, and medications. I was held there until they decided that I was no longer a danger to myself.

The time I spent there was humbling. Case-in-point: Being visited by my wife and daughter in a mental hospital is not something I ever care to remember. Granted, it was so nice to see them each day during "visiting hours," but I can only pray that my daughter was young enough for it to be a memory which quickly faded away as just another unremarkable and unmemorable anomaly of life.

I was surrounded by people with whom I had no desire to interact. I spent my time reading the book *The Visible Man* by Chuck Klosterman, a book about a therapist treating a brilliant and disturbed man who invented a suit to make him appear invisible. I felt invisible in that hospital, sitting in the corner, away from the generalized insanity surrounding me. The carpet was coarse and stained and the place smelled like a dilapidated museum; and each person on display and exhibiting their own unique affliction, be it schizophrenia, suicidal tendencies, bi-polar disorder, chronic depression, or the unknown. When I wasn't reading, I was silently observing. I never interacted.

Having a bachelor's degree in psychology, as well as having worked in the mental health for a few years, I knew the catch phrases and key words to use (and not use) that would make the doctors think that I was fine. I played them and manipulated them, just like I'd done with most of the other people in my life for a majority of my existence, telling them what they wanted to hear so that I would get what I wanted from them — in this case, so the shrinks would think I was stable enough to leave. And, of course, it worked. I was there for less than a week.

The story about me hit the Wichita news the same day I swallowed that bottle of pills, and by the time I was released from the hospital and sent home, plenty of viewer comments had accumulated on the websites of the various news stations. *And I read every single one.* All of them. And this was probably the worst thing I could have done, but it really brought me back to reality and showed me just how much of a villain I'd become — the things being said about me by people whom I'd never met were so vicious and atrocious, it almost seemed like hyperbolic satire. But these people were 100% serious. The worst comments were on the KAKETV article, which featured a picture which was both inflammatory and deceiving (showing toy A-B-C blocks and crayons, making it seem as though I'd done something to an infant or toddler). And while I fully believe my actions were atrocious, portraying my actions in the incorrect context was irresponsible and inflammatory. Regardless, this was the world in which I now lived, this was the context in which I now lived. So instead of depression, I sought redemption.

Positive Infamy

I decided that if I was going to be known for something like this — if my name was going to be "out there" for what I'd done — perhaps it could serve some good. I had long-regretted my actions, but never did anything proactive other than to keep living and teaching with propriety. So now that I'd been exposed, I decided to take things in a different direction.

I've always been inspired by a man named Frank Meeink.[94] He wrote a book entitled *The Autobiography of a Recovering Skinhead* in which he detailed his life as one of the most dominant and violent skinheads on the East Coast.[95] But after being arrested and sent to prison, his perspective on life completely changed, and he now spends his life speaking to different groups, talking about how hate and racism are destructive, corrosive, and dangerous.

Essentially, he was part of the problem; he became part of the solution. And that was precisely what I wanted to do. I came up with this idea I called "The Silhouette Initiative," in which I was willing to speak to teachers, educators (or anyone, really) about the epidemic of teacher-student relationships, providing the unique insight of someone who was once part of the problem, but was trying to be part of the solution. And it was certainly a good thing to do, but deep-down, I needed to do it for me. I felt like I'd done so much bad that I needed to do something good — I needed balance. I could not have cared less about how it made me "look" to want to do that, I needed redemption for the evil I'd spread throughout my corner of the world.

---

94   As a result of writing this book, I actually got to meet him.

95   The film *American History X* is partially based on his experiences.

However, the educational community would hear nothing of it. I was met with complete rejection and ridicule. For reasons I will never fully grasp, I was told (repeatedly) that this was my way of blaming the education system for the choices I made. Somehow, people translated my suggestions of preventative measures as me attributing fault for my own actions to not being trained properly, or something. In retrospect, much of this was possibly said out of spite, but that does not change the fact that my original idea for "The Silhouette Initiative" was flat-out rejected. And yet, even in the face of this rejection, I still spent that entire summer writing about the issue on the website I created for it, as well as publishing several early-draft chapters of this book online. I wasn't seeking publicity, I was seeking redemption. I felt a driving necessity to fix what I'd broken, and since there was no way I would be able to take back what I'd done with my former student, the best I could do was attempt to prevent it from happening to another student in another school, by another teacher, somewhere.

This was me, figuratively standing up, dusting myself off, and trying to move forward.

CHAPTER SEVEN

The morning of November 2, 2012, seven months after my arrest, was the start of a day that represented the culmination of preparation, stress, and strategy. It was my sentencing hearing. The day was cooler than usual, but not cold; generally unremarkable and extremely average.

Having lost our home in Lawrence, my wife, daughter, and I had moved back to Wichita and were living with my dad and stepmother. There is something shamefully humbling about being in a position where the most viable option for a place to live with my wife is in the room where I grew up. My parents were gracious enough to give us a place to stay, but that didn't make the shame any less plaguing. My actions had forced my family to move in with my parents. This is a very painful reality.

I woke up that morning feeling normal, with just a dash of stress. I have one memory that is absolutely burned into my consciousness: My six-year-old daughter came into my room and gave me a big hug before she left for school, and I hugged her just a little longer. I knew my hearing would start before she got home from school, so there was a good chance that this would be the last time I would hug her for the next five years. It was a very difficult feeling for me to comprehend.

She walked out of my room and down the hall, skipping along on a rainbow of oblivion and naiveté, having no idea that Daddy may be taken away in just a few short hours.

A few months earlier, I stood up in court and pled guilty to the charges against me in a pre-arranged plea agreement with the district attorney. I was guilty. I knew it, my attorney knew it, the prosecutor knew it, and everyone in my life knew it. I denied the charges against me the night I was interrogated, but that was clearly a falsehood. Otherwise, I'd been very straight-forward, honest, and transparent about what I'd done. There was no use in hiding anything anymore and I was tired of playing the game.

My original grossly-inflated charges[96] had been amended downward to two counts of aggravated indecent liberties and two counts of indecent liberties. And under the plea agreement, the two aggravated charges were dropped and I was to be sentenced on the two counts of indecent liberties, each carrying a penalty of thirty-two months in prison. Thus, the worst-case scenario would send me to prison for about five years. And on Friday, November 2, 2012, I would learn the disposition of my fate and future.

As a part of the plea agreement, my attorney was allowed to seek probation as a "downward departure" at my sentencing hearing, but he could not (for some reason) seek less prison time.[97] Thus, when I walked into court that day, I would either leave at the end of the hearing, going straight to the probation office, or I would be taking a

---

96   Again, this is a fairly common (and shady) tactic by the police and district attorney's office. When a suspect is arrested and initially charged, the authorities levy the most severe charges possible. This is done for two reasons. First, it makes for great press in a sensationalizing media culture that thrives on the downfall of others. And second, when the district attorney finally gets around to amending the formal charges, which are less-severe than the original charges, it carries the sleazy appearance that he (or she) is doing a favor for the person being charged. This, in-turn, leaves little (or no) room for defense attorneys to negotiate a lesser plea because the district attorney simply reiterates the point that he's already decreased the charges, which was his intention from the get-go.

97   I never understood this, but then again, we're dealing with the "justice" system.

five-year break from liberty and freedom. Obviously, the former was a bit more appealing to me than the latter.

Sentencing Hearing

When I sat down at the defendant's table in the courtroom, my attorney sat down with me and we waited quietly. I looked up in time to see a few people wheeling in a large television attached to a DVD player. My Attorney, Jess Hoeme, and I were confused and he had no idea what was going on. He immediately stood to go ask around, but from his body language, I gathered that no one would let him in on the presentation. Initially, I thought perhaps Taissa had pre-taped her statement to be played in court. And just about the time I considered this possibility, I turned to tell my wife — who sat right behind me in the first row of the courtroom gallery — what I thought was going on, and that's when Taissa walked in.

She didn't look like I'd remembered. She was a natural blonde, but her hair was dyed auburn, and she'd put on some weight since the last time I'd seen her several years prior. We didn't make eye contact and I didn't look in her direction for very long. I didn't want to antagonize the situation because, walking in behind her like a protective big brother, strolled Detective Virgil, minus the creepy mustache and looking about ten years older and twenty pounds lighter than I remembered.

The air was suddenly palpable and everyone seemed to notice. For the first time, the accuser and the accused were in the same room. It was as though the tension could not only be felt, but heard in a loud and silent melody — not with some sort of dramatic melancholy tune; it was heavy and intense, like the opening guitar and drum riff of Marilyn Manson's "The Beautiful People;" as though we were all about to stand up and fight it out, *Mad Max* style, and everyone was moving in slow motion.[98]

---

98   Granted, I'm sure this was just my own perception of the situation.

It felt like a battle was about to commence, and while I wanted to stand up and partake, I could only spectate. But I knew people would be fighting for me. My attorney was sharp and smart and I had a lot of confidence in him. He was ready, like a sniper, fully prepared to take aim.

The prosecuting attorney walked in and gave me a smug look that made me want to set him on fire. As the two sides were preparing to clash, another development was occurring behind me. As I was subtly scoping the courtroom, I noticed all three of Wichita's television news stations setting up cameras behind the courtroom gallery seating, and conspicuously seated in the empty jury box was a photographer from the Wichita Eagle newspaper along with a reporter grasping a hand-held notebook.[99] I was hoping to be old news, but the truth is, I was a sex scandal and people would certainly tune in to see it.

Numerous members of my family drove to Wichita to support me during the sentencing. My wife and parents were there, of course, but my aunt and uncle and several cousins drove to town as well. Ironically, at what seemed at the moment like the lowest point of my entire life, humiliated on television and preparing to face a judge for the worst choices I'd ever made in my life, I was surrounded by members of my family who were showing me unconditional love. It was nice to know there were people like that still in the world.

The judge walked in and the proceedings began. My adrenaline spiked and didn't calm for the entirety of the hearing. I wish I'd been more naïve or ignorant of the situation at the time it was taking place, but the truth is, I was fully and completely aware of the gravity of what was occurring before me. I knew that my immediate and not-so-distant future depended on the outcome of this hearing. I was hoping and praying for probation, but deep-down, I just knew it wasn't going to happen. With every in-town network zooming their cameras

---

99   As it turns out, my sentencing took place the Friday before Election Day in 2012, my sentencing judge was running for re-election, and we were all about to be on television. So this was like a free campaign commercial for him. In retrospect, I was screwed regardless. But not completely.

in, there was no way I was going to walk out of that courtroom in anything except shackles.

Testimony Begins

The first person to testify on my behalf was a psychiatrist who'd done a mental health evaluation on me. He testified about how I had an above-average IQ and was more-or-less normal, but was likely struggling with depression during the time of my crime and about how the relationship between Taissa and me coincided with the only difficult time my wife and I ever struggled with during our marriage.[100] He also talked about how I struggled with going from the single college guy life to the life of a husband and father, and then struggled with the pressures of graduate school and a full-time job and a family. He made some good points, but all-in-all, he didn't really seem like he wanted to be there. And then the prosecutor cross-examined the therapist.

"Don't lots of people deal with the same pressures as Mr. Brundage?" he asked.

"Yes," the psychiatrist replied.

"You would agree with me that millions of people have exactly the same problems in their everyday lives who don't commit sex crimes against children?" the prosecutor said sardonically.[101]

"Yes," the psychiatrist said mechanically.

"And you're familiar with Mr. Brundage's suicide attempt in March?" the prosecutor asked.

"Yes, I am," the psychiatrist replied.

"And to your knowledge," he said, pausing to dig through a stack of papers on the podium in front of him, "was that his only suicide attempt?"

---

100   My choices were in no way my wife's fault. This was simply another factor contributing to my own cognitive distortions.

101   Apparently, in this prosecutor's world, everyone handles pressure and depression the exact same level-headed way. Right.

"To my knowledge, it is," the psychiatrist said.

And that's when I silently gasped. I hadn't told the psychiatrist about what I'd done with the sleeve of my shirt as I sat in jail the night I was arrested, tying it around my neck, wanting to die, hoping to choke myself to death, but failing. The prosecutor knew about it because I'd written about it and published it on the "Silhouette Initiative" website several months prior, and he (of course) had a full print-out of all of it.

I didn't hide it from the psychiatrist during his examination of me; I guess it just never came up and I certainly didn't volunteer the information because I wanted him to assess me as being as level-headed as possible. Granted, we spoke in-depth about my overdose, but he never asked me if there were "other" times that I'd tried to harm myself.

My train of thought at the moment was interrupted by an awkward silence. It seems that the prosecutor had gotten ahead of himself and asked the question before he'd had his direct quote in front of him, and after he asked and the psychiatrist answered, he stood there, digging through a disorganized stack of papers, trying to find something that had seemingly vanished. Thus, his incompetence had turned his initial question into some sort of innocuous confirmation of information, when it could have been a blow to my credibility. Thank God for incompetence.

And then, after digging through his haphazard stacks of paperwork, the prosecutor proceeded to blow my mind. From the bottom of his paper mess, he pulled out an essay that I'd written in college ten years earlier; a satire piece I'd written about how there was homosexual and pedophiliac imagery in the movie *Willy Wonka and the Chocolate Factory*.[102] He immediately began to read excerpts

---

102 It took me a long time to figure out where he'd gotten this paper, because I was sure that he hadn't gone to my university and questioned my professors. As it turns out, the paper was stolen from a notebook that I kept in my classroom of my old college papers and essays for my students to reference if they wanted ideas or to see what I'd written in the past. The student who stole it was a boy who was himself a homosexual, and was offended by its contents. So, he stole it and made a copy, but then did nothing with

from the paper (taken extremely out of context, of course) which painted me as some sort of sex-obsessed pervert. But my attorney was on it. While the prosecutor stood up there reading, Jess was on his iPad, and with a few quick searches on Google, he was ready.[103] So when he did a re-direct questioning on the psychiatrist, he had a few questions.

"Have you ever heard this theory about that movie?" my attorney asked the psychiatrist.

"Seems like I've heard something like that," he answered.

"Well, I just Googled it, and it seems like a couple hundred thousand other people have had the same theory. Does that surprise you?" Jess had a slight smile.

"Not at all," the psychiatrist replied.

"In fact, he may have plagiarized some of it," my attorney said. "It's definitely not an original idea."[104]

"I don't believe so," the psychiatrist replied.

Then, as the psychiatrist remained on the stand, the prosecutor turned on the big-screen television and put a disc into the DVD player. I was glad we'd gotten to this, simply because I was genuinely curious what was going to be shown on this big television. And then I heard the music.

A few months earlier when I was working on my "Silhouette Initiative" project, I came up with the idea of making a little promotional video and uploading it to YouTube and putting it on the website I'd designed.[105] It had some news coverage about me and about

---

it until I was arrested, at which point he gave it to his grandmother who gave it to the police. Go figure.

103 Seriously, Jess is a sharp attorney. I was lucky to have come across him. If not for him, my prison time would have been doubled, or worse...

104 Ego made me want to tell him that I certainly didn't plagiarize it, though I did do the research behind the theory. But he was the attorney and I was the client and he knew best, so I just let him roll with it.

105 In retrospect, I think I spent the time making this video as a way to keep my mind productively engaged during that summer between my arrest and my sentencing; again, I needed to feel like I was doing something positive.

other teachers who'd been convicted of doing what I'd done — and worse — and culminated with the idea that someone needed to be the voice that brought the issue to the forefront of the conversation. And for reasons which still escape me, the prosecutor decided to try to use this video against me.

Jess Hoeme, my attorney, knew I'd been doing this, and he thought it was an excellent idea as far as keeping me occupied and productive in the months before my sentencing, but he'd never really considered using it during my sentencing because it would have looked like I was doing it for the mere purpose of trying to get a lighter sentence. And personally, I was fine with him not using it at my hearing; I wasn't doing any of it to make myself "look good." But when the prosecutor brought it up, Jess was nothing less than thrilled. In fact, about two-thirds of the way through the video, he leaned over to me and whispered, "This is freakin' great!"

And he was right!

As the video concluded, the prosecutor turned to the psychiatrist like a hungry lion staring at an unsuspecting gazelle. The psychiatrist's expression didn't change.[106] The prosecutor started asking some harmless questions — "Have you and Mr. Brundage ever discussed this?" he asked, shaping his eventual question.

"Yes."

"Why did he say he wanted to do this?"

"To help people, I imagine."

"He's going to use this to make money, isn't he," the prosecutor said, turning to look at me as he spoke to the psychiatrist.

"I think that's a reasonable assumption," the psychiatrist replied.

Ouch. Suddenly, I looked like a guy who was trying to exploit my own crimes for money. The prosecutor was trying to remove all altruistic motives I had. That one hurt. All I could do at that point was

---

106 In fact, I don't think it ever changed. I seriously don't remember him altering his facial expression at all, it was like watching a talking bearded mannequin.

hope my attorney had a few solid retorts when he subsequently cross-examined the psychiatrist.

"Did Mr. Brundage ever say that he wanted to make money from this?" Jess asked the psychiatrist.

"Not that I can recall," the psychiatrist answered.

"Was there anything on his website that indicated any sort of financial charges?"

"None that I know of," the psychiatrist replied.

"Well," Jess said, "is there anyone better-suited to deliver this message?"

"Not that I can think of," the psychiatrist replied.

"Mr. Brundage appears to want to try to keep others from making the choices he made, would you agree with that?"

"I would," they psychiatrist replied.

"Do you think his motives are genuine?" my attorney asked.

"Yes, I do," the psychiatrist concluded.

After a brief pause, the psychiatrist stepped-down and my wife was called to the stand. The prosecutor approached her like a con man targeting his next mark. "So, let's talk about this 'Silhouette' project Mr. Brundage has going," the prosecutor said.

"Okay," she said in her sweet and melancholy voice.[107]

"Why do you think Mr. Brundage wants to do this?" he asked.

"I think he just wants to make some good out of a bad situation," she replied. She had the slightest wavering vibration in her voice that made it sound like she was on the verge of tears, but was afraid to show emotion.

"And does he want to make money by doing this?" the prosecutor asked as though he was accusing *her* of something.

"No, he doesn't," she replied.

"How do you know this?" he asked her.

---

107 The moment she spoke on the stand for the first time was extremely difficult for me. I remember the horrid feeling of knowing no husband should ever put his wife through what she was currently experiencing.

"We talked about it," she said. "He said that if anyone wanted to help pay his travel costs or something, he wouldn't mind, but he said he didn't want to be paid for it."

"Then how would he support your family?" he asked.

"Well," she said, now visibly a little annoyed at this man, "I have a college degree and a full-time job."

"So, you would work and he would just travel around for free?" he asked in a very sarcastic, rude, and unprofessional tone of voice.

She paused and gave him a very stern look, as though she was scolding a preschooler. "Sir," she said, "we are a family and we are in this together."

To this, he did not reply. My attorney stood up for his cross-examination.

"Is Kurt a good father?" he asked her. I think that was the first time I'd heard my first name used during the testimony.

"Yes," she said proudly, "he is an excellent father."

"Do you guys have a good relationship?" Jess asked.

"Yes, we do," she said. I think she may have smiled slightly when she said it.

It was nice to hear, I suppose. I'd done so much to hurt her, all out of selfishness and addictive compulsion; yet there she was, testifying in a court of law, that we had a good marriage.

Sometimes, hearing your wife tell a judge, under-oath, that she loves you, can mean a lot.

After she testified, my mother testified about how much she and the family needed me around and about how she'd just had surgery and was depending on me. She also said some positive character things and did her best; my father also submitted a similar letter to the judge — but it was all about to wrap-up.

My Statement

I was then given the opportunity to speak in my own defense, so I stood up and began reading my attorney-approved statement:

In January of 2010, I made the biggest mistake of my life. I fully admit that the things I did were completely wrong and there is no excuse for what went on. These actions have had a profound effect on my life as a person ever since. These events occurred during the only rough-patch that my marriage has ever faced. I was spending entirely too much time on my career and rarely saw my family. My priorities were out of order in nearly all aspects of my life. So, when someone expressed an attraction to me, I made the wrong decision and did not attempt to stop it. Since she had transferred to another school and I did not see her on a daily basis, I made the mistake of allowing myself to view her as a peer rather than a former student, leading me to blur the line of propriety in order to gain the sense of affection that I was missing from my own marriage. At no point was her age a contributing factor.[108] And although these interactions only lasted a few weeks, they will plague me for the rest of my life.

Not long after these events took place — in the late winter of 2010 — I confessed to my wife what I had done,[109] and the two of us made the decision to recommit to each other and strengthen our marriage by reconnecting with our Christian faith. This effort culminated in August of 2010 when we were both baptized together, making the decision that our marriage and our lives would be lived according to our beliefs. Our marriage has grown stronger by the day ever since and I have tirelessly sought God's forgiveness for the events that took place.

---

108 When I said this in court, I emphasized it, because it was completely true. At no point was I ever attracted to her "because of" her age. I never had that creepy "I want an underage girl" thing. I just began to view her as a peer, and since my boundaries with my other peers were lacking (at best), the situation unraveled out of control.

109 ...along with a whole lot of other things I didn't need to mention in open-court. Because seriously, if anyone knew what was actually going on with teachers in high schools, everyone would homeschool their children.

Since these events have come to light, I've lost my career, my home, and most of my friends. My wife and daughter must now live with the stigma of having me for a husband and father, and most of my closest friends, including the best man at my wedding, will no longer speak to me.[110]

I have expressed my deepest remorse to the victim ever since things ended two years ago, and would continue to do so, given the opportunity.

I am, from the bottom of my heart, truly sorry.

To her parents, who put their trust in me, I am also very sorry for letting you down. I would also like to apologize to my former colleagues and students. I betrayed my profession in the worst way and violated their trust as well. To my parents, who have been loving and supportive for these past seven months, I am deeply sorry that your son ended up in this situation; this is my failure as a person, not your failure as parents. And to my wife, you are the rock upon which I build my life, and I see the love of God in you. Your forgiveness is what has kept me afloat during this horrible time.

Moving forward, I want my downfall to benefit others. My wife and I have formed what we have entitled, "The Silhouette Initiative." Unlawful teacher-student relationships have become an epidemic that is occurring entirely too often. As a teacher, I was never once given any education or direction on how to keep from falling into this type of situation. The goal of "The Silhouette Initiative" is to go into the community and educate teachers, administrators, parents, and future teachers in college about this epidemic, how to keep the walls of propriety solid, and what to do when these difficult situations arise. My website explains — in detail — what my wife and I are seeking to do to help remedy this on-going problem in our schools. As

---

110 Partly my fault for what I did, but mostly because he's just an arrogant, selfish, self-important, self-absorbed tool.

a father, I would be horrified if my daughter's teachers ever did what I did. So, if I can use my experience to keep this from happening to someone else, then this situation that has hurt so many can perhaps help even more. My wife and I have prayed extensively about this, and we both feel that God is leading us to become a voice for this cause, to keep this from happening to others. I cannot change what happened, but perhaps I can keep it from happening to someone else, somewhere else, in the future. This problem is only addressed after it happens.[111] *That needs to stop. Thank you.*[112]

And then I sat down.

Her Statement

And then *she* stood up. It was Taissa's turn to read her pre-written statement. She was standing about ten feet behind me, and I sat up to turn around in my chair, and Jess, my attorney, grabbed me and I froze.

"Do–not–turn–around," he whispered slowly in a stern hush. "Just sit there and look sorry." And considering he was the attorney and I was the client, I complied.

I must be perfectly honest, I didn't listen to a single word she said. I *couldn't.* The sound of my hectic breathing and the petrified pounding of my heart were drowning out any coherent sound around me. I could hear, but I couldn't hear anything. Her voice hit me like the intense psychological music from a horror film, meant to scare the screams out of people as they stare at a blackened screen.

---

111 I stand by this statement. Granted, it should be common sense and shouldn't need to be mentioned. But if that was truly the case, it simply would never happen. But it happens all the time, and most of the time, the teacher gets away with it. I know of at least two, and probably three.

112 In retrospect, I loathe this statement. I feel like I still didn't take enough responsibility for what I did and I can definitely see how it seems like (in this statement) I blamed the system somehow – but this was never ever my intent. I simply worded the statement poorly.

I couldn't hear her over the sound of my own fear.

"For the last two-and-a-half years," she read from her prewritten statement,[113] "he got to go on while I was being stalked by the memories of these things that he had done to me." She talked about how she had difficulties being in a room alone with another adult male. "The entire time I've been sitting here,"[114] she read, "listening to everything, everyone refers to it as a relationship. But I see a relationship as being something where two people are in consent. When one person is not in consent, I don't consider it a relationship."

And then she sat down.

Sentence Rendered

And then it was the judge's turn. I was ready to hear the judge tell me that I would be going to prison for sixty-four months, thirty-two months for each count. This judge — on the Friday before Election Day, an election in which he was on the ballot; in front of cameras from all three Wichita news stations; a photographer and reporter from Wichita's only newspaper — would never grant me probation.

And he started talking. And he talked some more. And I don't remember a single thing he said until I heard a number. *Thirty-two.* So I started listening. Until that moment, it had been my assumption that my two options were either probation or the full sentence for both counts. And then another word caught my ear: "concurrent." In his dialogue, the judge decided that I needed to do time, but that the full amount wouldn't have been necessary, so he met everyone in the middle and gave me half the time I expected, thirty-two months.

---

113 My only recollection of her statement is what I read in the newspaper a few days later. So, this is not her statement in its entirety; only what was printed in the Wichita newspaper.

114 To be perfectly honest, when I read this line in the newspaper, it bothered me a little. This was a pre-written statement she read in court. So using the prepositional statement, "The entire time I've been sitting here," just struck me as disingenuous. I have no doubt that she felt this way; I suppose I was just bothered by the delivery.

This meant, with good behavior and program-credit, I would serve twenty-five months at best.

My attorney stood up and asked if I could have a day or two to get my "affairs in order" and that was promptly denied. I was told that I would only have a few minutes before I would be taken away — to prison.

Farewell

I turned around and sadly gazed upon my wife; she was crying. It was probably the most painful thing I've ever seen. To look into the eyes of a woman just before her husband is taken away to prison; it sent a shock of emotional agony through my soul — a shock I hadn't felt since the night I first told her about my infidelity. And as I turned to scan the faces of those who'd come to court to support me, I saw that similar depth of empty agony in the eyes of my loved ones as well. It's a tough moment in life when you realize people hurt *for* you and *because of* you at the same time. Wow, that hurt. I couldn't think of anything to say to any of them that would matter, so as each one hugged me goodbye, I said the only thing I could think of: "I'm sorry." And I was. I was sorry they'd come to court; I was sorry they had a reason to come to court; I was sorry they had come to court *with* me and would be leaving *without* me; but most of all, I was sorry that I'd let them all down.

It was time. I turned to Jess and shook his hand, thanking him for all he'd done, and I was promptly handcuffed to be taken down and booked into jail, again. It would be the last free air that I would breathe for the next two (plus) years. And as I heard the handcuffs click around my wrists and felt the cold metal against my clammy skin, I turned and gave my wife one last glance that said "I love you" and "I'm sorry" in one melancholy gaze. The pain in her eyes which dutifully replied shattered my heart.

And with a sad poetic sense of finality, I was promptly escorted from the free world.

CHAPTER EIGHT

spent two years, one month, and three days in prison. That's 763 days. That's 18,322 hours. That's 1,098,720 minutes. And I felt every — single — one. But the most painful of those 18,322 hours happened within the first 60.

The judge handed down my sentence in court and graciously allowed me the chance to hug my wife and family goodbye before being escorted by a Sedgwick County Jail Deputy through a door in the courtroom behind the jury box; a door that led into a long ominous back hallway — a door that led back to Hell.

Welcome Back . . . to Hell

The hallway was long and tortuous — or at least, it seemed that way, like the back hallways of the Bellagio in *Ocean's Eleven*. And when I was finally guided by the wordless jail deputy onto an elevator, I knew instinctively we would be going down. Because according to lore, that's the figurative descent into Hell; according to the layout of the County Courthouse, that's the literal descent into jail.

The elevator doors closed with an uncomfortable *clank*, and the elevator itself sounded labored as it did its best to lower my temporary and momentarily-automated casket toward Dante's Inferno without dropping us into the fiery lake of burning sulfur.

When the doors opened, I was escorted to a heavy thick automatic sliding door, and when I walked through, it closed behind me as I stood before an identical door. The last time I stood between these same doors, I was facing the other way, on my way home after being bailed-out, the night of my initial arrest. But this time, I would not be leaving.

There was a span of several torturously long moments between the closing of the door behind me and the opening of the door before me, like being in the airlock of a spaceship, knowing the comfort and safety of the interior was behind me and the chaotic unknown void awaited.

The escorting jail deputy stood silently, like a moving statue. In fact, he didn't say a single word for the entirety of our journey downward. He was my escort to the Underworld, like Charon, the mythical "Boat Man" from Greek Mythology who carried newly-deceased souls across the River Styx. The deputy's facial expression never changed — an unmoved expression of either boredom or apathy; or both, or neither. He couldn't possibly care less that I was heading to prison. I was nobody to him and his level of give-a-crap was nonexistent. It was my first and most profound lesson about prison: *"You do not matter."*

I could see through the door's thick window in front of me as I awaited its inevitable opening: The booking area of the County Jail. I'd been here before. And as the ominous heavy door opened, breaking the uncomfortable silence between Deputy Boat Man and me, an invisible and uncomfortable mist filled the airlock.

I remember reading in a college psychology class that smells and scents are the biggest triggers of memories. As the brain processes scents and memories, smells get routed through the olfactory bulb, which is the smell-analyzing region in the brain. It is closely connected to the amygdala and hippocampus, brain regions which handle memory and emotion. And trust me, being in jail the first time created quite an emotional memory. So, when that familiar smell — that odor — wafted into my nostrils again, I knew — and remembered — exactly where I was.

I was reluctantly escorted to the familiar chest-high green(ish)-blue(ish)-puke(ish)-colored desk and essentially dropped-off by Deputy Boat Man. He promptly retreated through the airlock without a word and vanished into the archives of my experience. The desk deputy gave me a look, seeing that I was standing there in a tie and glasses and looking somewhat sophisticated and dressed up, and motioned me toward an awaiting deputy behind me who would walk me to my holding cell — he motioned with his chin and head, apparently not willing to put forth the effort of raising an arm or extending his index finger, let alone using actual words. And before this third deputy put me into the holding cell, he took my tie and my belt, asked if I had a watch, wallet, or wedding band (which I didn't, having given them to my wife in the courtroom before being removed from the Free World). He then escorted me to a corner cell with ten or twelve other people waiting on benches to be either transferred to the housing units of the jail or bailed-out.

I stood in the doorway of the holding cell as the heavy door slammed behind me and locked with another ringing thud of finality. No one appeared to look up from their conversations or snoring to see that a new contestant had entered this dejected contest of life-failures. It only took a fraction of a second to realize that I looked like a complete idiot standing there, so when I saw that there was an open corner, I quickly but casually made my way toward it and staked my claim. I sat down on the floor, pulled my knees to my chest, and hid my face from my inevitable future — my only thought being, *Life can't possibly get any worse.*[115]

---

115 Imperative Lesson: Never tell Life, "You can't possibly get any worse," because Life will promptly reply, "Challenge accepted!"

There is no feeling of failure which equates to that of sitting in jail, knowing the next step is prison. It far exceeds the feeling of failure at a specific task. Sitting in jail, awaiting prison, I knew I hadn't failed at a mere task — I'd failed at *life*.

After remaining motionless in my self-constructed ball of solitude for a few hours, a deputy opened the door and said my name. "Brundage," he called in an apathetic monotone, holding a small index card. I stood up and walked with him back into the open booking area, not asking why or where or how or what or anything. He motioned me toward a very overweight and hairy man wearing old gray sweatpants, an AC/DC shirt, and a jail employee name tag; he sat behind a curtain in what looked like a cheaper version of a high school nurse's office. And as I went in and sat down, I knew precisely what it was, having been through the same drill when I was initially arrested. This was the health screening; part of the booking process. He asked me about my basic medical history, drug use, tobacco use, alcohol use, etc. My answers were mindless and unremarkable. Then he asked about mental health.

And I should have lied.

"Are you feeling depressed right now?" he asked.

"I'm heading to prison, so I'm not exactly thrilled," I replied with as much sarcasm as I could muster-up (which, admittedly, wasn't much — I sounded more like a petulant jerk).

"Have you ever attempted suicide?" he asked. I was a little bothered by the manner in which he asked this question. This particular inquiry had a lot of weight to it, especially considering what was about to happen to me, not to mention the severity of the act itself, but when he asked, he might as well have been asking me if I was allergic to peanuts or cats.

"In March," I said matter-of-factly, "I swallowed a bottle of pills." I paused. "But clearly I'm still here."

The gargantuan hairy guy in the AC/DC shirt, who looked like he'd just finished his janitorial shift somewhere, didn't even look up when I sardonically indicated that my life had reached such a depth that I'd tried to end it. He simply moved on to his next innocuous and inane question before indicating that I could go back to my holding cell. There, I would await transfer to the residential section of the jail.

Suicide Watch

I sat back in my corner of the holding cell, but was only there for a half-hour or so before another deputy, one I had not yet seen, came to the door and called my name. "Brundage," he said in a nearly identical monotone voice as the last deputy. I again stood and followed him, no questions asked.

We walked through the open area and out a door leading to a hallway, leading to another hallway, leading to a room which led to another room. The room where we eventually ended up looked like an abandoned locker room, and it certainly smelled the part.

"Strip search," the deputy said. I expected this and began to reluctantly and uncomfortably disrobe. He took each article of clothing, checking them for contraband and personal items, and subsequently bagged them to be sent home. And when I was fully disrobed, standing before him, completely naked and utterly humiliated, I waited for him to complete his paperwork and put his clipboard down so that I could be given the cliché County Jail jumpsuit.

But that's not what happened.

"Here," the deputy said as he put down his clipboard. He extended to me a large piece of heavy material with sleeve holes and Velcro. I had no clue what this thing was, and the look of confusion on my face prompted an explanation from the deputy.

"You're being put on Suicide Watch," he said.

Wait, *what*?!

I was speechless. And I think he picked up on my bewilderment because he somewhat immediately explained.

"Policy is, if you've had a suicide attempt within the last year, you're automatically put on Suicide Watch." He spoke as though he was telling me how to change my windshield wipers; to him, it was no big deal.

I took the odd green heavy Velcro smock from him and held it in front of me, naked, trying to figure out how I was supposed to put this awkward heavy thing on. I was contemporaneously growing more and more agitated and confused the more I thought about the fact that I was being put on Suicide Watch, even though I wasn't suicidal.

"So, who determines that I'm *not* suicidal?" I asked as I uncomfortably examined this one-piece heavy smock.

"The mental health nurse on duty," he replied.

"Can I talk to her?" I asked with staccato in my voice. "It will take like 30 seconds for her to realize I'm not suicidal, at all."

"They don't work weekends," he replied casually.

"So, she'll be back Monday?" I asked. I could feel how wide-open my eyes were.

"Yep."

It was 9:00PM on Friday night.

I paused and stared at him, hoping my facial expression and silence would convey: *a)* how upset I was about this; *b)* how irritated I was that he didn't seem to care; and *c)* how utterly ridiculous it was for a correctional facility to not employ any mental health staff on the weekends.

"Fine," I said, refusing to make eye-contact with him. I fastened the heavy green smock over my shivering and humiliated naked body, and stood motionless — barefoot and furious — awaiting my next instruction.

He led me down another hall to an open jail pod and into a cell specifically for Suicide Watch. I entered the cell, feeling simultaneously enraged and defeated. The door closed behind me and the thud rang for an eternity.

This was really happening.

The Abyss

So, I stood there in the middle of this one-man cell and evaluated my surroundings. There was a metal toilet attached to a metal sink, the floor was stone and cold, the walls were brick and stone, the bed was metal and cold — and had no mattress. Suicide Watch precautionary measures remove anything that a person could use to cause harm to himself, including clothing, all personal effects, and anything in the cell that is not bolted-down. There wasn't even toilet paper. And to add to it, they took my glasses. I'd worn my glasses to court in a shallow attempt to look smarter, so when they took my clothing from me, they also took my glasses. I couldn't see a single thing.

When I sat down on the cold metal slab which would serve as my bed, I thought to myself — *nothing*. I could think *nothing* and I could see *nothing*. But I could hear other inmates congregating in the commons area of the pod; I was not allowed out of my cell. There was only one light in my cell, and it flickered like a dull indecisive and inconsistent strobe light. And I literally couldn't form a fully-functional cohesive thought.

But I could still feel. And at that moment, I felt the metaphorical *thud* of my entire life finally hitting rock bottom, sinking to the deepest valley of this Abyss.

I looked around, let out a sigh, and laid my head down on the metal slab. But after trying several positions without any comfortable success, I stood up and walked to the door of the cell, pressing the button that paged the desk deputy on the cell's intercom.

"What," the deputy said without inflection.

"Can I have a roll of toilet paper?" I asked.

No reply. I pressed the button again. Nothing.

Then, the door unlatched and swung open. An apathetic hand thrust a cheap roll of toilet paper into the cell. "Let me know when you're done," he said in a clear *I-don't-care* tone of voice.

"I can't keep it?" I asked.

He paused and looked at me like I was being high-maintenance. "Fine," he said, shutting the door briskly.

But the truth is, I didn't need to use the toilet. I needed a pillow.[116]

When I returned to the metal slab bed, I unfastened the Velcro on my heavy green smock and used it (as best I could) as a blanket to cover my body. I turned onto my side, placing the roll of toilet paper under my head, and curled up into as much of a ball as I could, trying not to move. I had to grit my teeth until the cold metal against my naked skin was warmed enough by my body heat to keep my body from shivering uncontrollably. If I moved, the cold uncovered metal jolted me like an icy shock.

After several hours, I finally drifted off to sleep. But it didn't last long. I woke up repeatedly, each time thinking it was all a nightmare from which I would soon be pulled back to civility. Not the case. The nightmare was my reality — a reality I admittedly deserved. And each time I happened to find a shallow bit of slumber, my body would shift and the cold metal on my leg or my hip or my arm or my shoulder would jolt me awake again.

I had no way of knowing what time it was; there was a clock far-across the pod from my cell, but as I looked out the cell door, I squinted as hard as I could and still couldn't read it. They took my glasses. I was trapped, helpless, sightless, sleepless, and frigidly cold. I could only curl myself into a ball and do my best to cocoon myself between the heavy fabric of my green smock and the agonizingly cold metal slab bed.

I have no idea what time it was when they brought me breakfast. According to my window,[117] it was still dark outside when I was served my morning meal. I got up and looked at it, and I literally could not identify it. Seriously, I have no clue what was on that tray. It wasn't

---

116   Yes, I was forced to use a roll of toilet paper for a pillow. This was my life now.

117   The window was more than eight feet from the ground, so even standing on my metal slab bed, I still could not see out; I could only judge the amount of light shining (or not shining) into my cell.

moving, thankfully; so, there's that. It may have been grits, perhaps, but it looked and smelled more like the liquefied corpse that Walter White and Jesse Pinkman dissolved in acid on *Breaking Bad*. This was breakfast. No thanks. I didn't eat. I dumped it in the toilet and left the empty tray by the door, returning to the safety of my cocoon.

When the sun finally came up, the noise of the jail pod awoke me from whatever brief bout of sleep I'd managed to find. And it wasn't long before my mind began to race. The depression turned to stress and the stress had me pacing the tiny cell in my heavy green smock and bare feet.

The more I paced, the quicker my steps became and the room kept getting smaller and smaller and colder and colder and louder and quieter and the ringing in my ears and the fleeting thoughts in my mind never stopped and I kept getting exhaustively energized and frustrated and depressed and angry and I paced and paced and paced until the bottoms of my bare feet became sore and my naked shoulders became chafed from the Velcro that rubbed and scratched my bare skin which was only made worse by the cold sweat that covered my entire body and made me even more cold which made me shiver more and my face became sore from clenching my cheeks and grinding my teeth and all I could do to alleviate the stress and the pain and the despair and the depression was pace the room until I had no energy left in my body.

And that's how it was for me, in that little cell, all day. I was never even let out to bathe.

Lunch, like breakfast, was delivered on a clunky tray and was barely identifiable. I tried to eat, but couldn't. I had no appetite, no desire to eat, no desire to even sustain any sort of nutrition whatsoever. I knew I needed to eat; my body was telling me it needed nutrients, but I simply couldn't bring myself to shovel this mystery sludge into my mouth. It smelled like something left-over from dinner — *six weeks ago*. But honestly, I didn't care. I wasn't going to eat it. I seriously began to contemplate whether or not death-by-starvation would be a painful way to put myself out of my misery, if death meant being able to leave that cell. Because in all honesty, I was fine (though upset) as I sat in that first holding cell, waiting to be transferred to the residential area of the jail. *But I wasn't suicidal.* I wasn't even contemplating death — I was merely daunted by the two years of prison awaiting me; I'd spent the previous months preparing myself for the possibility. But staring at the "meal" they gave me, I could only wonder if starving to death was painful, because I couldn't think of anything *more* painful than being in that room. So, like breakfast, I dumped it in the toilet and left the empty tray to be picked up.

Ah, the irony: I hadn't even contemplated death or self-harm or suicide until I was forced into Suicide Watch.

At one point, they wheeled a television out into the open area of the pod, and the film *Training Day* was on. I›ve seen the movie numerous times, so although I could not see the screen, I could hear it. And since the only opening between my cell and the open pod was the space beneath my door, I curled up in my cocoon on the floor and listened to the sound of the movie as it crept under my door and into my cell - I watched the movie in my mind.[118]

That movie is the last solid categorical memory I have of being on Suicide Watch. Granted, I have other recollections, but they all seem to mesh together into one huge cacophony of cognitive clusters. Hours felt like days and time stopped. Well, not literally, but at one point, time literally did go backwards; I was in jail during the first weekend in November. *Fall-back.* It was Daylight Savings Time. And in a place where an hour felt like a long and endless day, adding another hour to my solitary confinement was just a cruel joke.[119]

It was always dark in my cell, except for the flickering light. It always smelled musty with a hint of odor from the toilet that clearly hadn't been cleaned since Jimmy Carter was president, so I was

---

118 I have not seen that movie since, and likely never will again.

119 While locked away, I literally had to live one hour, twice.

reluctant to use it. And in a cell of stone and metal, it seemed to somehow radiate with varying degrees of cold. In Dante Alighieri's *Inferno*, he describes the deepest depths of Hell, not as a fiery burning lake of sulfur, but as a bitter cold wasteland, devoid of God. And those two attributes described my surroundings perfectly: It was bitter cold, and God was not there.

Of all the places I've been and all the things I've experienced, that was the first time I'd ever been anywhere — at any time — and literally felt like God was *not* there, because *He wasn't*. I honestly believe the time I spent in that cell was the first (and hopefully only) time God has chosen to turn His back on me.

Time stopped. For days, time stopped. I could only base a general estimation of the time on what meal was being brought to me (though I didn't eat them); however, at one point I expected lunch and got breakfast, which was my biggest indication that I was beginning to lose the only firm grip on reality I had left.

Sanity Again

And then, on Monday morning, it was over. A woman came to the window of my solitary cell and began asking me questions.

"How are you feeling?" she asked.

"Fine," I said.

"Do you have any thoughts of hurting yourself?" she asked.

"No," I replied. "None."

"Okay," she said.

And then, the door opened, I was handed a Sedgwick County Jail jumpsuit, and led to the residential area of the jail. And just like that, with a few well-placed lies, I was released from the Abyss.

I was escorted to another elevator, then through another maze of hallways, and then told where I would be going for the time-being.

"Pod Ten," a faceless deputy said as he herded me toward the barracks-style pod. I was carrying a standard-issue set of sheets and a blanket. They don't give out pillows at the County Jail, but they can be rented. And once I got to Pod Ten, I saw that the mattresses were the same disgusting worn bed pads that were in the holding cells. Disgusting? Yes, but at least it was a mattress. I was thankful for a mattress. So, I was assigned a bed and told to put my things down and go shower. Yes, shower. I was thankful for a shower.

Finally, my ordeal in that particular circle of Hell was over, and I was thankful to begin my climb out, with or without Dante and Virgil's assistance.

After getting showered and situated, I was — for the first time — allowed to use the phone.

I called my wife.

And at the very instant I heard the sweet sound of her voice, I wept.

I wept because within the beautiful sound of her voice and the loving embrace of her words, God had returned to me, and I felt Him next to me again.

And still, I wept.

After three weeks in jail, I was shipped off to prison.

763 days.

That's 18,322 hours.

That's 1,098,720 minutes.

And I felt every — single — one.

CHAPTER NINE

So, fast forward five years. On a gloomy August day in 2015, I was a 35-year-old man living with my parents, sleeping in the bedroom I grew up in, unable to live at home with my wife and daughter; the state decided my charges somehow automatically meant I was a danger to anyone under the age of 18 and I was therefore prohibited from having any contact with any minor, including my own daughter. The fact that I'd never hurt my daughter — *ever* — was irrelevant to them. It took nearly a year of living as much of a "normal" life as possible before I could convince the powers-that-be at the parole office that I wasn't some sort of sick predator. Of course, over time, my actions would categorize me as the lowest-risk parolee on their caseload, but initially, it wasn't quite that simple.

Ruined Lives

Life's gray clouds hovered ominously on that gloomy August day, and it seemed as though they were there to stay. My father did his best to keep my spirits high, but there was very little he could say to ease the sting of being forcefully kept from my wife and daughter. I had, at that point, at least earned visitation rights — *supervised* visitation rights — but I could not spend the night in my own house where my wife and daughter lived. We were not allowed to be a family.

This is what a ruined life looks like.

No one ever seems to contemplate what the lives of these teachers — *us* teachers — looks like *after* all the headlines have passed and sentences have expired. It becomes out-of-sight, out-of-mind and the bitter results of the (much-deserved) consequences are easily overlooked and forgotten. It simply isn't an aspect which is thoroughly contemplated by anyone outside of the situation. When the dust settles, life must still go on, though a ruined life it may be.

I was fortunate enough to have several career options after my release from prison, as well as an exceptionally-strong support system of family and loyal friends.[120] But as I've found from talking to numerous people, this is a rarity for anyone convicted of committing a sexual offense. There is less of a social stigma held on someone who commits murder than someone who commits a sexual offense. For example, there is a prevalent assumption that all sex offenders are pedophiles. Yet, according to the United States Department of Health and Human Services, only 34% of sexual offenses involve a victim under the age of twelve, and over half of all sex crime victims are over the age of eighteen. Another assumption is that anyone convicted of a sexual offense is "sick" and "incurable," which is also a fallacy. While there are certainly sexual predators who are deeply pathological, not all offenders are somehow "sick" or mentally ill — many simply made very poor and tragic choices.

But in this realm, facts do not matter. The shameful label is there and it will never — ever — be erased. My sex offender registration requirement lasts 25 years. But I don't pretend to think the stigma will suddenly disappear once I'm no longer on their website. So, while the

---

120 It is important to mention here that my loyal friends were few. Most friends – including my life-long best friend – deserted me, and several members of my family will have nothing more to do with me either. In fact, my own cousin mocked me online relentlessly after I was interviewed by the Wichita paper before speaking at a national conference. But still, I consider myself fortunate.

years may be numbered, the reality is infinite. It's a brand, a tattoo, a scar that will not go away — a *Scarlet Letter*.

However, this all pales in comparison to the impact it will have on the student with whom I had a relationship. Throughout the time I spent in and after prison trying to put my life back together, I have been very certain not to forget or minimize the impact my choices had on Taissa. She did nothing wrong and did not deserve what happened. What happened with Taissa didn't happen *because* of her age, it happened *regardless* of it, and I believe that is every bit as dangerous. She was just another woman to me, and I essentially ignored everything else because I viewed her as a peer, not a student, so age simply was never a factor.

This is the foundation of this epidemic.

Most teachers are not having relationships with students because they are attracted to high school students; they are having relationships with students because they are viewing the students as peers — equals — rather than products of their occupation. Thus, when the lines of authority are blurred, the lines of propriety can easily become blurred as well.

Cognitive Distortions

Many teacher-student relationships are not a result of a mental illness, they are a result of a drastic *Cognitive Distortion*. A psychiatrist named Aaron T. Beck initially studied this concept and eventually wrote a book called *The Feeling Good Handbook* in which he explores, among other things, how a person can experience Cognitive Distortions — thought patterns which are irrational and/or exaggerated, and which lead to a subtle (yet powerful) altering of a person's perception of their own personal reality as well as the reality around them. Essentially, Cognitive Distortions are thoughts which lead a person to perceive reality inaccurately, often based on personal experiences. This concept is the foundation of reason when explaining why teachers have relationships with students.

Entertain this concept for a moment: Many teachers who have relationships with students are not attracted to them because they are teenagers; they are not attracted to them because of their youthful age. Is this a concept that is difficult to accept? Is this a path of logic that seems unbelievable, almost to the point of ridiculousness? Most people would agree. It is a general perception among the public that teachers who have relationships with students are doing so because they have some sort of deviant sexual attraction to individuals of a very young age.

Now, try this perspective: These teachers are not becoming attracted to students because they see them as children; teachers are becoming attracted to students because they see them as adults. A fine line, perhaps; but *this* is where the concept of Cognitive Distortion begins to take shape.

Faulty Syllogism

I once read a comprehensive study which stated, "Men who shave on a daily basis tend to live longer." This statement, initially, seems a little ridiculous. If judging this one statement purely on the merits of the information contained in the sentence, the implication would be that shaving on a daily basis somehow extends men's lifespans — as though there was something about the act of removing facial hair regularly which enabled the human body to live longer. And this, of course, *is* ridiculous. Men who shave on a daily basis tend to live longer — but the simple act of shaving does not make a man live longer. Upon deeper analysis, it is shown that men who shave on a daily basis have better grooming habits, and men with better grooming habits are more likely to take care of their overall well-being (such as health, diet, and appearance), which leads to a healthier lifestyle as-a-whole. Thus, men with a healthier lifestyle tend to live longer. This makes much more sense than the original statement from the study. Therefore, although *Factor-A* and *Factor-B* tend to coincide, it does not automatically mean *Factor-A* caused *Factor-B*, and *vice versa.* This, in any context, is a very errant assumption, known as a "faulty syllogism."

This concept has never been more evident than in the contemporary political climate. Individuality and original thought have taken a backseat to an assumption that everyone must identify themselves by who they voted for in the previous election or who they plan to vote for in the next one. And a subsequent side-effect of this mindset is to assume anyone with whom we disagree is automatically on the "other side." Many Republicans assume most black people in "the ghetto" are Democrats — many Democrats assume most white people in "trailer parks" are Republicans.

Just because *Factor-A* and *Factor-B* tend to coincide does not automatically mean *Factor-A* caused *Factor-B*, or *vice versa* — a faulty syllogism.

So when a teacher has an inappropriate relationship with a student, a very similar process evolves. The general assumption is that sexual crime is driven by sexual motives to quench some sort of deviant sexual satisfaction or desire. But what if — *just, what if* — this is the exception rather than the rule? What if the underlying motives of teachers who cross the lines of propriety with students are actually much more complicated, complex, and convoluted? And what if sex — the actual act and motivation of sex — has little (or nothing) to do with it?

Admittedly, this may be a difficult reality to accept (or even grasp). But until the correct issues are addressed, the overall problem will not be solved. And since the problem persists, the educational community must concede that their efforts have been unsuccessful thus far and they must seek further differing theories.

James Spader, speaking as big-time Boston attorney Alan Shore on the television drama "Boston Legal," made a comment during Season Two which perhaps struck at the heart of the issue. His supervisor, played by Candice Bergen, tells him his constant pursuit of the younger women attorneys at the law firm make him seem "sad" and "pathetic." She asks him, "What is it about young women? Is it simply a matter of improving blood flow?" Clearly, her assumption is that his motives are purely sexual. But that is not the case. And in a somber moment of self-reflection, he replies, "I'm not so much attracted to younger women. It's more the idea that they could be attracted to me."

The most vital and operative word in Spader's quote is *not* the word "younger," it is the word "idea."

That brief scene, from an episode of a television drama originally broadcast on October 25, 2005, paints the perfect picture of why high school teachers are having relationships with students. Of course, the issue is still much more complex than this, but essentially, "It's more the idea that they could be attracted to me" sums up the motive of many teachers who cross those lines of impropriety.

The foundation of this issue is not built upon perversion or predatory drive or deviant desires — the foundation is built upon a genuine sense of latent emotion. These teachers — *we* teachers — who have crossed these terrible lines are emotionally-broken people. It is painfully evident that the demonization of these teachers solves nothing, simply because no one else feels they themselves could possibly be a member of this demonized category. So, just for a moment, humanize these teachers — view their actions as choices driven by complex and faulty emotions; view them as people, not monsters. *That* is how to solve this problem. No one thinks they could ever become a monster, but humans are fallible and often make terrible choices. But it is more comfortable to label these teachers as "sick" than it is to consider them human.

The Comfort Zone

In the film *Se7en*, starring Brad Pitt, Morgan Freeman, and Kevin Spacey, there is an interesting (and relevant) conversation which takes place near the end of the film between Brad Pitt's character, Detective Mills, and Kevin Spacey's character, a serial killer referred to only as "John Doe."

"I've been trying to figure something, in my head," Detective Mills says to John Doe as they're driving in their car, nearing the climax of the film, "and maybe you can help me out, yeah?" John Doe gives Detective Mills a sideways look. "When a person is insane — as you clearly are — do you know that you're insane?" His snarky tone is only matched by his subtle arrogance. "Maybe you're just sitting around," he continues, "reading 'Guns & Ammo,' masturbating in your own feces; do you just stop and go, 'Wow, it is amazing how f--king crazy I really am!' Yeah? Do you guys do that?"

Quite a scathing question to a serial killer who *is* clearly insane. And yet, his retort is grounded in reason. His retort, when genuinely understood, makes more sense than the question to which he replies.

"It's more *comfortable* for you to label me *insane*," John Doe says matter-of-factly with a confident grin.

"It's *very* comfortable," Detective Mills replies immediately, with confidence and surety.

And *that*, in a nutshell, is a significant part of the problem.

When another high school teacher is publicly arrested and charged with having another relationship with another student, the public (as well as teachers and parents and even other students) point bitter accusatory fingers and scream things (both literally and figuratively) like "pedophile" and "sicko" and "pervert" and "rapist." These words are at the extreme-far end of the spectrum regarding the issue offending teachers may or may not actually be encompassing. However, it is "more comfortable" to label them as being "pedophiles" or "perverts."

Therefore, the solution to this problem is found *outside the comfort zone*.

CHAPTER TEN

The educational community is light-years away from actually solving the problem of teacher-student relationships. After everything that has happened, the correct and appropriate people are still not asking the correct and appropriate questions. It is easier to hastily and hatefully point fingers at teachers who cross those fateful and tragic lines, but when it comes to preventative measures, there is simply nothing being done, even by those who are responsible for protecting the well-being of students.

Before effective steps can be taken toward addressing this issue, the question of motive must be answered.[121] However, in the case of teacher-student relationships, it is just as important (if not *more* important) to emphasize what the problem is *not*, because as it stands, assuming the motive for these behaviors is caused by some other force leads to addressing the problem inadequately and incorrectly — and the problem will not be solved. Therefore, identifying the correct cognitive distortion and ignoring the unrelated hype-driven

---

121 Please be clear: Nothing I am saying or will say in this chapter - or this book (or ever), for that matter - should be misconstrued as a "justification" or "excuses" for the behaviors of teachers who cross the lines of propriety. The purpose is to provide an in-depth (and logical) perspective regarding why these lines are crossed.

assumptions should be the goal of anyone who seriously wants to address the issue.

"Just be careful..."

Here is a perfect example of how school districts are *not* attempting to prevent this problem: My wife is a teacher and during her first year of teaching, all new teachers spent an extra week before other teachers were required to report, going to in-services and trainings for New Teacher Orientation. And, being conscious of the issue herself (after all, she's *my* wife), she kept waiting and waiting for something to be said about the issue of teachers and students becoming "too close" or having inappropriate relationships. Days and days of trainings and meetings and in-services passed, and nothing was said.

Finally, someone in a meeting managed to circle around to the issue. The speaker, nearing the end of his presentation said, "And you high school teachers, you're not that far apart from the students in age, so, you know, just be careful."

That was it.

That was the only thing she, as a new teacher, heard from anyone — at all — during her orientation. And here's the kicker: It wasn't even a school district employee who said that; it was a guy from the Teacher's Union. He did not make this statement as a representative of the school district; he said it during his pitch to get new teachers to join the Teacher's Union. So, essentially, the school district itself — the largest school district in the state, the same school district where I taught when I committed my crime — had *nothing* to say to new teachers about teacher-student relationships.

The one remark I hear the most regarding this issue is,[122] "Well, it should be common sense for teachers not to have relationships with students." I agree; I completely agree; I couldn't agree more! But clearly it's not, because it's still happening — *all the time.* So if the

---

122 ...other than the remarks directly ridiculing me for my own choices regarding this issue...

mere assumption that it "should be common sense" is the extent of school districts' attempts at preventing this from happening, then they are, by default and neglect, putting students at risk.

The First Question

But what can be done? How does a school district prevent teachers from pursuing inappropriate relationships with students? That's the million-dollar question, but it's not the first question that should be asked, and that's the problem. School districts, principals, and even other teachers are seeing a problem and are asking how to solve it. But that cannot be the first question.

The first question must be: *Why is this happening?*

The problem *is not* that teachers are having relationships with students — that is the *result*. The actual problem is much more in-depth, much more complicated, and much more uncomfortable than that. Teachers and school administrators can no longer afford to assume that this is an insulated or isolated issue, specific to only the weird, sick, bizarre, mentally-ill teachers who happen to become mistakenly employed.

It is easier and more comfortable to cast horrific labels on horrific acts and only assume it is because horrific people are making horrific choices, plain-and-simple. Countering upon the possibility that good people can make bad choices makes many people uneasy, uncomfortable, and unusually anxious. After all, if good people are capable of evil, then anyone — any "normal" person — is capable of evil; this is not a comfortable notion to consider. So the human comfort zone includes the instinctive reaction to casting horrific labels on horrific choices.

But why? Why would casting these horrific labels on horrific acts actually be "more comfortable" for a person who perceives themselves as "normal?" The answer to that is simple, and it's an answer I learned in prison.

Racism in prison is rampant, but oddly enough, it's not about race — it's about behavior. When I was in the county jail, spending several weeks waiting to be shipped off to prison, a guy in jail with me (who'd been to prison before) said, "If you're not racist before prison, you will be after prison." I wasn't quite sure what that meant, seeing as how I grew up with black friends and didn't have a racist bone in my body. But then again, he'd been to prison and I hadn't so I just figured I'd wait and see. But when I got there, I noticed something: Whites hated blacks, but blacks didn't necessarily hate whites. But after talking to some of these racist white guys in prison, they expressed that their hatred of black people was based on their behavior — things black guys did which these white guys found disagreeable. So one day, I flat-out said to one of these racist white guys, "You don't hate those guys because they're black, you hate them because you don't like what they're doing or how they're acting; so what you're doing is, you're trying to find a way to conceptually separate and distance yourself from them so that you can take comfort in the fact that you're as different from them as possible. And the easiest way to do that is to find the most obvious manner in which you differ from them, which is, in this case, the opposite color of your skin. Basically, you're taking the *main difference* between the two of you — skin color — and making it *the main reason* why you dislike them." He didn't quite track this logic, and frankly, I wasn't surprised. "You don't like them," I said, trying to simplify the issue, "so you're taking the most obvious thing that separates you two and making it the reason you don't like them."

He still didn't get it. Oh well. But my reasoning was sound, and it is the same logic behind the reasons people are comforted by shouting "pedophile" and "pervert" at teachers who have relationships with students. By seeing their actions as the biggest difference between them (rather than the underlying problems and issues), teachers and parents can put up a social and moral barrier between themselves and the offending teacher by using these terms of extremity. However, the truth is actually much more unnerving. And that's where Cognitive Distortions come into play.

Blurred Perspectives

In the contemporary American workforce, workplace sexual affairs have almost become commonplace; I should know, I had numerous affairs with numerous other teachers when I was teaching and many of my peers were engaging in similar behavior.[123] Teachers often become engrossed in their teacher social circle, blending their social lives with their professional lives by having drinks with co-workers after work or meeting up on weekends for social functions. And of course, there is nothing wrong with this behavior and it can be very beneficial to creating a comfortable and cohesive work environment.

However, there comes a point when the lines and perspectives begin to blur — and it all begins with social acceptance. Teachers, like most professionals, want to be respected and appreciated. However, teachers often seek respect from their students as well as their colleagues. There have been many studies which support the hypothesis that students learn better from teachers they like and respect, both as educators and as people. Fostering a positive personable image as a teacher (rather than merely being a rigid educator) can be a valuable teaching tool for teachers. But it is certainly a slippery slope. Gaining "likability" from students and connecting with them on a deeper level opens the door for non-curriculum conversations such as sports, music, movies, television, etc. All of this is innocent bonding; discussing things like pop culture with students can be beneficial and many studies would indicate that it is actually encouraged — students will often refuse to learn from a teacher who is perceived as "out-of-touch."

When I taught, my students knew that I was an avid runner and a baseball fan, they knew what music I liked, what movies were my favorites, what books I read, etc. As an educator, it provided a personal

---

123 Obviously, the quantity of these occurrences did not make them permissible.

depth beyond simply being a teacher, and students were responsive to the notion that they were learning from a "real person" and not just a robotic educational statue, programmed to recite facts about Shakespeare and grammar.

As far as teachers are concerned, students should be viewed as one thing — and one thing only: A product of their occupation — a work product. Student achievement and student success is Priority #1. "Getting to know" students is not a necessity beyond knowing what is needed to help them succeed in academia. *Students are work products.* Being viewed as a "regular person" should be used simply as an academic strategy, not a social status mark.

However, for some teachers, the script flips. As teachers seek to be viewed by students as "regular people," those same teachers sometimes begin to view their students as "regular people" as well. The social discourse is a two-way conversation, so as students learn a teacher's likes and dislikes, the students express their own, adding depth to themselves as well. And the slope grows more slippery by the second.

Peer to Peer

When students start seeing teachers as regular people, studies indicate they are more apt to learn from them. But when teachers start viewing students as regular people, history has shown they have a tendency to view them as *peers* rather than *work products.* The adult sees the teenager as an adult peer rather than a subordinate student. And this line is only further blurred by the multiple mediums of communication.

Teachers begin giving out their cell phone numbers and allowing students to text them; teachers begin "friending" students on Facebook and allowing students to "follow" them on Twitter; teachers begin allowing students to send them messages on Instagram or Snapchat or any number of social media outlets. At that point, the student has ceased to be a student and has become a peer. So why is it any surprise that so many teachers blur the line between teenage peer and adult peer, subsequently viewing these teenagers as adults? And when two peers, perceived as adults to one-another, become attracted to each other, why is society shocked and surprised when that first kiss happens and a relationship ensues?

In the day and age when emails reach our phones just as quickly as text messages, there is really no feasible reason for a student to have a teacher's personal cell phone number. The teacher may see it as only a means of communication with little-to-no differentiation between text messages or emails or Facebook messages, etc. However, the student does not see it that way. The student sees access to a personal cell phone number or a social media connection as a deep and personal view into the life of the teacher. They live in a time when social media is as personally intimate as a face-to-face conversation, whereas many adults view social media as a simple way to connect with people and post a few vacation photos.

Therefore, assuming the teenager can view these things through the same lens as an adult is to assume the teenagers are adults themselves — this is another tragic cognitive distortion. Perceiving teenagers as peers (or adults) through social or peer-like interactions only precipitates the possibility of inappropriate contact.

Social Hierarchy

Another significant predicating factor which leads to the crossing of boundaries between teachers and students is the teacher's insistence on being a part of the students' social hierarchy. It is human nature (for the most part) to want to be liked, respected, even admired. However, many teachers take this concept beyond logic by wanting to be viewed as the "cool" teacher by the students in their classes (or even not in their classes), and this mindset is one of the first variables which begins to murky the waters of propriety.

In researching the many cases of unlawful teacher-student relationships, this was a recurring theme of many of the disgraced educators. They were well-liked, popular, and "cool" teachers; rarely was the disgraced teacher "odd" or "creepy" or "weird." Far more often than not, it was a respected, well-known, attractive, young teacher[124] who crossed the line of propriety with a student.

Essentially, this is the other end of the spectrum. Rather than the adult cognitively distorting the teenagers as fellow adults, they are distorting themselves as teenagers. For some teachers, it's their chance to be popular in high school again, or for the first time. In this instance, the teacher isn't attracted to the student because the student is a teenager, but rather the teacher is viewing him/herself as a teenager, part of the social hierarchy of the high school status quo. But again, the teacher is not attracted to the student *because* of age, but *despite* it.

When a teacher inserts him/herself into the students' social hierarchy, the teacher crosses from professionalism into personalism, which is an area no teacher should be, with the exception of very few extenuating circumstances. However, understanding that there are no absolutes, it is safe to say that a high school teacher has no place in the friend zone of his/her students. And while it is fine (and even beneficial) for teachers to provide their students with a little more depth of personality,[125] when a teacher begins to seek status with students, that is the beginning of the gray area.

The fact of the matter is this: Right now, for all of those "social" things, a vast majority of teachers, principals, school officials, and school districts turn a blind eye to social interactions; nothing is done, and no one seems to care — until that first kiss happens.

The unassuming fact school administrators need to realize is this: Anything beyond basic teacher-student social normality is off-limits. There is no viable reason for a student to send a teacher a text message.

---

124 Male or female. It is important to note that the disparity of numbers between male teachers and female teachers who cross the lines of impropriety with students is not as wide of a gap as media coverage would imply.

125 For instance, favorite sports teams, musical preference, marital status (if married), children, etc. These details add depth to a teacher, making him/her more relatable.

There are always other alternatives. And there is absolutely no reason for any student to have any social media interaction with any teacher at any time. If this is not the policy of a school and/or school district, then that school district is practicing gross negligence and should be liable for legal repercussions.

Admittedly, I was guilty of breaking all of these norms. That's not to say this is why I did what I did — I made my own choices — but as far as perpetuating circumstances go, it was certainly on the list. But one important lesson can be drawn from this: This is a warning sign — an indicator — that a teacher is either having an inappropriate relationship with a student or is setting him/herself up for the possibility in the future, either perceptively, intentionally, or inadvertently. When teachers begin viewing students as peers rather than work products, the chances of an inappropriate relationship increase from *improbable* to *possible*.

CHAPTER ELEVEN

To truly address the issue, the examination must go deeper than just interactions between students and teachers. The overall improprieties create a culture that turns a blind eye to misbehavior by teachers and creates a culture of permissiveness regarding an array of unethical and unlawful behaviors.[126]

Here are a few examples: During my first week as a teacher, there were no students. The first week of every school year is full of meetings, trainings, in-services, and classroom preparation time. Oh, and drinking — *lots and lots of drinking*. Mornings were relatively low-key, mostly filled with mind-numbing meetings and pointlessly redundant training sessions, but when the lunch break came around, the party started. And this was nearly every day.

Liquid Lunches

For our lunch breaks during in-service days, teachers were allowed to leave the campus for a little over an hour and get lunch wherever

---

126 Allow me to once again reiterate this point: I do not blame the "culture" I describe for my choices. It's not other teachers' fault that I did what I did and I do not blame them – I blame me. However, these points about the culture among the teaching staff are valid and explain why the issue of unlawful teacher-student relationships are increasingly occurring and are increasingly ignored.

we desired. And during this initial week, every lunch was spent at some sort of sports bar or cantina or anywhere that served booze. The first day, when members of the English department invited me to come with them to lunch at a place called The River City Brewery, I thought it would be a good chance to get to know my co-workers and introduce myself a little more through conversation. What I was not ready for was this: When the ten-or-so of us sat down and placed drink orders with the waitress, *everyone* ordered beer (or bourbon). And, of course, wanting to fit in as well as I could, I followed suit. But the thing is, it wasn't just a casual beer with our burgers. It was beer, then more beer, then more beer. By the time we needed to return to the school to begin the afternoon in-service sessions, everyone was excessively liquored-up. If the police department conducted breathalyzers in the East High parking lot, we all would have gone to jail on DUI charges.

And while we, the English department spent our lunches drinking, the Social Studies department spent their lunches making Bob Marley look like Michael W. Smith. The amount of marijuana consumed by members of the Social Studies department was incomprehensible, even to me. There was just something about history or psychology teachers that coincided evenly with smoking pot. It was often difficult to distinguish the Social Studies Department from a start-up reggae band.[127] But granted, the drug situation among the teachers certainly was not limited to the Social Studies department. In fact, to my knowledge, the only department that didn't have anyone who actively and enthusiastically did drugs at any given time during the school day was the Mathematics department; marijuana was mostly the Social Studies department, with more than a few members of the English department and a few sporadic members of the sciences dipping in as well. But everyone drank.

---

127 One Social Studies teacher (with whom I had an affair) used to sit at the back of her classroom during her hour off and smoke a joint, blowing the smoke out the window.

And all of this was done with the full knowledge of our bosses, the administration. One lunch during a mid-year in-service day (during my third of fourth year, I think), a big group of us went to lunch at a nearby restaurant called Margarita's Cantina and we, of course, all ordered giant margaritas (because, well, that's what you do at a place called "Margarita's"). And true to form, we pounded them down like mineral water in the dead-of-summer, rendering ourselves relatively wasted in a relatively short period of time. And as we sat at our big table drinking (perhaps fifteen minutes into our lunch, and likely on our third margarita), two of the assistant principals walked into the restaurant and got their own table across the room from ours. I thought for sure we were busted. We would certainly be told not to return to school in any kind of impaired condition. I thought we were in deep trouble. And I thought this, until I glanced over and saw the two assistant principals being delivered their own jumbo-sized margaritas.

A Blind Eye

A few years later, while I was serving as an administrative intern[128] at Wichita East High School, I was walking the halls with a walkie-talkie, listening to the chatter between the security staff and the administration. It was the annual day when the Wichita Police Department brought in the drug dogs to sniff-out the school, trying to bust the dope-smoking demographic of the student population. They walked the halls, sniffing the lockers, finding a few dime-bags here and there, and then went out to sniff the cars in the student parking lots.

As I was listening to the back-and-forth radio traffic between the administration and the security staff, one of the security officers told the administrators that the dogs had just finished sniffing the seniors'

---

128 This is the principal version of student-teaching while I worked on my Master's Degree in Administration.

parking[129] lot and were going to make their way to the juniors' and sophomores' parking lots. In order for the police to make the most direct walk from the senior parking lot to the juniors' parking lot, then the sophomores' parking lot, they would need to cross through one of the teachers' parking lots.

"We're done with Senior Lot," I heard one of the security officers say on the radio, "and we're taking the dogs to Junior."

"Security," the radio said in the voice of one of East High's assistant principals, "*do not* take the drug dogs through the teacher parking lot!" He paused. "I repeat, *do not* take the drug dogs through the teacher parking lot!" He almost sounded panicked.

"Okay," the security officer replied on the radio, clearly and audibly laughing. "We'll walk the long way around." He was being accompanied by several Wichita police officers, who also complied and avoided taking the drug-detecting dogs through the faculty parking lot.

The administration was fully aware of the extensive drug use that was happening among the faculty during the day, and frankly, there was already a teacher shortage.

So, how does this relate to inappropriate teacher-student relationships? Simple: This type of blind-eye attitude from the administration (which is not uncommon across many schools of all levels) creates a culture of deviance. Unwillingness to hold teachers accountable for their actions, simply by looking the other way, creates a culture which (in a roundabout way) condones unethical behavior. School administrators cannot seemingly allow (by default) certain illegal behavior and then be completely surprised when other illegal behavior ensues. Essentially, don't be shocked when a teacher crosses the lines of propriety when they are not held accountable for crossing the likes of sobriety.

---

129 Each respective class had their own designated parking lot. Seniors had the best parking, followed by the Juniors, and then the Sophomores. Freshmen typically didn't drive, but in the event they did, they parked with the Sophomores.

Party-on, Wayne

On the weekends, the teacher parties dwarfed the student parties. There was an interesting dynamic at play when it came to accommodating the out-of-control partying behavior of the teachers. Every year during the first week of school, teachers were informed that they were required to attend two extra-curricular activities as sponsors or chaperones, and one specific one was required: Graduation. Thus, there were numerous options for teachers to choose in order to fulfill their other requirement, most of which were school dances.

There were three major school dances: Fall Homecoming, Winter Homecoming, and Prom. Sign-ups to chaperone these events were limited and were first-come-first-serve. There were two understandings amongst the faculty: First, the Fall Homecoming, the first of the three to occur, was more-or-less reserved for the older and more apathetic teachers who wanted to merely get their requirement done and out-of-the-way; second, Prom was reserved for the younger, boozing, drug-addled partying teachers because for the teachers, Prom wasn't so much about Prom, it was about the After-Prom. The Winter Homecoming dance and the few other random events were the catch-all for whoever didn't fit one of the first two categories.

The teachers who worked Prom made just as big of a deal out of it as the students did. Of course, we had to help set-up and tear-down the decorations, monitor the students, and keep order; but it wasn't just the duties. Teachers and their significant-others got into suits and dresses, we even danced, and more than half of us who showed up to work prom were drunk when we arrived from the dinner we'd just attended together. In addition, we subtly kept drinking throughout the night.

And the debauchery wasn't just chemical. One year, as we were all helping set up, trying not to ruffle our nice clothes, one of the assistant principals walked by the teacher who was in charge of organizing

Prom, saw her in her tight black dress, and said, "Damn, girl, when are you and me gonna go someplace dark?"[130]

And that's just how things were.

The teachers' After-Prom Party was an annual event. Teachers and administrators alike attended these gatherings and the supplies of alcohol and drugs were endless. One year at our After-Prom Party, I played a late-night game of beer pong with one of the assistant principals, but he thought using beer was weak, so he poured Jack Daniels in his cups. I won the game and about fifteen minutes later, he puked, impressively.

At the very first teacher party I attended, I dropped the gauntlet.[131] The party was at the home of an older (but still partying) teacher who threw the shindig for whoever wanted to show up for the booze and bonfire at her farm. So when my wife and I showed up, I had with me a 30-pack of Keystone Light and a roll of duct tape. People asked why I had duct tape, and I played it cool and mysterious in order to get as much attention as I could. So, in front of everyone, I chugged my first beer, then took the empty can, placed it under a full can, and duct taped the full can to the top of the empty one, cracked it open, and began to drink. And with every new beer I opened, I put the full on top and duct taped it to the stack. By the end of the night, I looked like an alcoholic wizard with my staff of beer cans.

This is just how things went — regularly. Nearly every Friday after school, a group of teachers met at a bar down the street from the school called The Anchor and got utterly wasted. And this bar was the closest thing I've ever seen to a hippy bar; the crowd was so ridiculously diverse, and yet, it seemed to work. There were guys with knit beanies and sleeve tattoos sitting at the bar next to guys in thousand-dollar suits. The place smelled like a blend of patchouli oil and Hugo Boss,

---

130 Seriously, he said this. Word-for-word. And it was just no big deal, although I'm not 100% convinced they didn't "go find someplace dark" sometime during the dance that night.

131 Once I'd firmly established that the partying teachers were the "cool" teachers (and I wanted to be one), I decided to deliberately do something memorable.

and the fragrance hovered over the greasy scent of burgers, onions, and sweet potato fries. But the amalgamation of aromas was neither off-putting nor pleasant; it just simply, *was*. And so, on Fridays, the hoard of khaki-and-t-shirt wearing teachers strolled in and claimed the same four or five tables, commencing the weekly liquid therapy. This is where the customary whining and complaining began as well, like the Festivus "Airing of Grievances."

I dove into the drunken revelry whole-heartedly. When I got the impression that being a teacher was — to a significant extent — about how hard I could party, I decided to throw my stock into the exchange and watch my investment flourish. There were two contrasting concepts: Booze and drugs. The drinking seemed like second nature, as though it was my responsibility and everyone who was anyone was a hardcore drinker.

The drugs, however, were different. More people were on drugs (marijuana, cocaine, pills, etc.) than I probably knew about, but what I did know was that everyone knew that it was heavily going on, but literally no one talked about it. It was always a wink-and-nod sort of thing. They talked in code, or just consulted a Thesaurus before conversing about it in an attempt to over-speak any layman who may be listening. But regardless, it was not uncommon to see two or three teachers subtly stepping outside to smoke a joint, or casually slipping into the bathroom for a line or two of cocaine, and Vicodin and Percocet were passed around like Tylenol. But that was simply the modus operandi of the teaching population. Teachers from other schools often showed up at our after-school bar as well, bringing with them their own array of drinking preferences and chemical enhancements. It wasn't uncommon for the principals to join in too, drinking just as heavily as teachers and acting every bit as foolish.

Often, two flirting teachers briefly left together, and no one said anything about what everyone knew; they would return later, blushing and disheveled. Even when it was known that they were married to other people, still no one said a word. Affairs between teachers were as commonplace as dusty textbooks and dirty chalkboards. It was a part of the landscape — part of the culture — everyone ignored. Sex in classrooms or in the parking lot of the bar was normal.

The sex and the drugs were things everyone knew about but no one mentioned, as though mentioning them would make the entire educational system come crashing down. And granted, not all teachers are partaking in this behavior — not even a majority. But it is enough to impact the overall school culture of many schools, large and small, rich and poor, public and private.

For me personally, these experiences solidified my routine and reputation among my fellow teachers as a partier, and it wasn't long before the booze-fueled partying brought along my own booze-fueled sexual affairs right along with it.

I look back on my out-of-control life as a teacher and I cringe.[132]

I had such a great opportunity as a teacher, and I threw it all away because I wanted to live a life I had no business living. I knew there were teachers who were drinking, doing drugs, and even having relationships with their students, so my own cognitive distortions led me to think that since others were participating in these behaviors, then it must be okay.

Reasonably Unreasonable

I must have asked myself a hundred times why my relationship with Taissa seemed like a reasonable option, but I remember one specific deluded thought: "I'm not the only one." Obviously, this is errant logic. There is no way I can possibly justify what I did by saying I wasn't the only one doing it. However, I believe my knowledge of the other teachers who were having relationships with students (or had in the past) gave me the delusion that somehow it would be okay. There were several. One teacher, with whom I was close friends at the time, was fired from his position as assistant girls' volleyball coach because of suspicions about him and one of the players. The wrestling coach

---

132 Seriously, sometimes when I think about it, I physically cringe or flinch.

resigned over allegations that he'd had a long-lasting relationship with a girl who was the student-manager of the wrestling team. The choir director at a school across town had a relationship with a student that was highly-publicized. The male orchestra director at my school actually married a former student whom he (officially) started dating almost immediately after she graduated. And yet, these were simply the *known* occurrences.

But there was one instance specifically which gave me the delusion that teacher-student relationships were the norm. One of the teachers with whom I was having an affair had a long-standing relationship years earlier with one of her students. Following one of our "after-3PM" liaisons, she told me all about how she'd had an affair with one of her students. He played in the school band, and she told me about the time the band was in Kansas City for some sort of performance, so she drove to Kansas City, got a hotel, and he snuck out of his hotel and spent the night with her. And apparently, word got around that this had happened, so the school and the police did an investigation that evidently yielded nothing. Like most of the illegal teacher behavior that went on at that school, the principal swept it under the rug and pretended like nothing happened.[133] And since *she* never got in trouble, something in the irrational part of my brain seemed to convince me that *I* wouldn't get in trouble either.

It was all part of the culture.

Again, this "culture" *does not* make teachers cross the lines of propriety with their students. However, this is simply one of many ingredients of a very dangerous recipe for disaster. When drug and alcohol use is permissible during the school day — around students, as I clearly observed (and regrettably partook) — why are people surprised when other boundaries are crossed as well?

Simply telling teachers not to have relationships with students is like a doctor treating a patient's symptoms, but not treating the

---

133 This sort of cover-up happened all the time. For example, there was an art teacher who was caught selling drugs to students, and she was given an "early retirement." Seriously.

underlying disease ("Yes, this Tylenol will help your headache, regardless of the brain tumor," the doctor would say). Therefore, to address this problem and correct this behavior, the overall culture must be changed — the overall context must be addressed. This problem will persist until it is sufficiently and accurately addressed.

CHAPTER TWELVE

was sitting in a restaurant once, on a date with my wife, enjoying the ambiance of the nice restaurant where we were dining, mesmerized by the cacophony of sounds filling the air — inanimate chatter, the clinking of silverware on porcelain plates, the tap of wine glasses being softly placed on the table after a gratuitous sip — my mind began to wander to whatever predominant notion was on my imagination at the moment. My wife had excused herself to the ladies' room and I sat at the table alone, essentially daydreaming. And as I stared-off into nothingness, contemplating this or that (essentially zoning-out my surroundings), I was snapped back into full consciousness by the sound of a plate breaking in the kitchen; and at that moment, I found myself in an awkward position. As I was staring into nothingness, marinating in deep contemplation, I had apparently been inadvertently staring at a gentleman across the restaurant, square in the eye. And when I realized this, I also realized his look of major confusion and mild discomfort as to why someone was staring at him. I was so deep in thought, I didn't even notice that I was staring right at him. Of course, I immediately looked away and made a feeble and transparent attempt at playing-it-off by picking up my iPhone and pretending to answer a text, but that did not remedy my embarrassment.

Moral of the story: Sometimes, we don't see the details of everything right in front of us, simply because of everything right in front of us.

Context...

I remember an interesting conversation I once had with a former student. I'd been out of prison several years and she was a senior in college at the time. And as we had occasion to catch-up, enjoying the banalities of a typical mundane conversation, she said something that prompted a deeper line of thought. As a twenty-two-year-old college student, she said, "There were high school kids on campus the other day, and they looked so small!" I, of course, laughed and agreed, but then she said, "I don't remember being that small when I was in high school." And that led to a more intriguing dialogue.

"Well," I said, "that was your context at the time. That was your *setting*." I paused, but received no retort. "Right now, you're surrounded by college students. That's your context — your setting — *now*. So, of course the high schoolers look small. Yeah, you've 'grown,' but not all that much. You're seeing them in the *context* of being high school students and your own mental predisposition[134] to yourself being 'older' makes you view them in a *context* of smaller."

"Hmm," she said in a syllable of contemplation.

"High school students didn't seem small in high school because that was your peer group," I continued. "They were neither big nor small nor old nor young — they just, *were*." I paused. "Context is *everything*," I said in an (admittedly) overly-declarative tone.

It occurred to me during this conversation (and even more-so afterwards) that this perhaps was a significant element of my own cognitive distortions as a teacher. To the average person, high school students look like high school students — annoying obnoxious know-it-alls who think they know everything while fully grasping nothing. But as a high school teacher, these annoyances were my context —

---

134 Yes, I actually use words like this in casual conversation.

my setting, my canvas, my work product — and it was the nexus of my professional existence. And my biggest mistake was my casual willingness to view them as social equals in my feeble and errant attempts at being the "cool" or "popular" teacher. Once I began to view high school students as social equals and attempted to insert myself as a variable of their warped social hierarchy, I was already on my way to blurring the lines of propriety.

Simply-put, I began to rate my status as a teacher by my popularity with the students, not my ability to effectively convey the content.[135]

If you drop a frog into a pot of boiling water, it will immediately hop out. However, if you drop a frog into a pot of lukewarm water and slowly but gradually turn the heat all the way up, the frog will boil to death.

I used this analogy in class all the time; the irony was, as I said it — over and over again, to class after class, year after year — I was the frog, steadily coming to a boil. And I didn't even see it coming. This, *obviously*, was never what "made me do it."[136] People who see this issue from such a black-and-white perspective either aren't intelligent enough to understand or simply refuse to understand that these situations aren't merely shades of gray, but a full pallet of colors. This isn't something I "blame" for my behavior. However, this is a mindset of which teachers must be fully-cognizant because it is much more common than one might think. Television shows and movies glorify the "popular teacher" while only sparingly making him/her also the academically strong teacher. So many teachers strive to be John Keating from *Dead Poets Society*, but instead end up becoming Harry Senate from *Boston Public*. There is an inordinate quantity of

---

135 In my opinion, this is the #1 problem with high school teachers today.

136 I must continually reiterate this point. Nothing "made me do it;" but the message keeps getting construed that way. There is an inherent need by the populous to assign blame to a person while ignoring all underlying variables; ignoring the variables upon which a situation is predicated is the most effective way to not solve a problem.

teachers currently in the profession who desperately seek popularity over educational effectiveness.

...is Everything

One conversation I had as a teacher — one I will never forget — was with a guidance counselor at the first school where I taught. He asked me (during my second year of teaching) how everything was going, and I think I made a half-comical statement about striving to be John Keating.[137] And his subsequent reply has *never* left my consciousness.

"Well, just be careful," he said, "because people always seem to forget that John Keating was *fired* at the end of that movie."

I've never forgotten that conversation, and yet, I would give anything to have fully-grasped it at the moment those words entered my psyche. Because he was absolutely right.

Being a teacher through the wrong lens is dangerous. Granted, it doesn't always end the same way my tale did, but it certainly happens all-too-often.

Context is everything.

And until we admit and acknowledge this one simple concept, many of these cognitive distortions will continue to ring true in the lives of teachers and bring strife to the lives of students.

Context is everything.

And until *all* teachers are willing to prioritize their educational effectiveness over their status of popularity with the students and staff, the quality of education given by teachers and received by students will continue to be lackluster and unproductive.

Context is everything.

Allowing oneself to become enveloped in a flawed context is dangerous because an altered context means altered norms. Norms exist for a reason — both customary and regulatory — so when those norms are ignored for the sake of an errant context, student

---

137 Robin Williams' character in *Dead Poets Society*.

achievement suffers, student safety is jeopardized, and tragic choices are made.

Never underestimate the power of context, especially within the context of school culture. When out-of-control and absurd behavior becomes the norm, context isn't simply everything, it becomes dangerous. Therefore, establishing solid and healthy norms in all aspects of educators' lives should be a top priority.

Great Teacher

There really is a disconnect between two basic factions of teachers and how the occupation is approached, regarded, and rewarded. Many teachers function in the mistaken context that teaching is about the teacher — it's not. Superficially, there is nothing wrong with saying "I want to be a *great teacher*." But the crux of that statement — that perspective — is based in the teacher him/herself, not the students. Being a great teacher shines the spotlight on the teacher and his/her teaching abilities, practices, and methods. But there is a deeper mindset there which seems to seek credit. And while teaching is sometimes a thankless profession financially, socially, and publicly, none of those things should be the reason a teacher becomes a teacher. Anyone who becomes a teacher for the money should really raise their standards.

While it is certainly nice to be recognized for being an impactful teacher, seeing oneself as a "great teacher" or being regarded as a "great teacher" is a subtle misnomer because teaching is not about teachers — teaching is about students.

So how does this mindset relate to unlawful teacher-student relationships? Simple. Anything in excess is dangerous. When a teacher wants to be a "great teacher" to the extent that image becomes more important than results, the overall set of priorities becomes skewed. Thus, when a teacher seeks recognition, he/she will seek it in whatever form possible, including friendships and popularity with the faculty, and even friendships and popularity with the students.

Too many teachers consider themselves to be "great teachers" by how popular they are with the faculty and students rather than judging their success by the academic achievement of their students. And unfortunately, this mindset has become dangerously commonplace and goes unaddressed (and is even sometimes praised).[138]

Teach Great

Perhaps the point-of-view should instead be, "I want to *teach great.*"[139] That was where I — and many — went wrong. Being a teacher was all about *me*. I relished in the praise I received on formal evaluations, or from peers, or from other teachers; all about how good *I* was at teaching. But instead of prioritizing how well I conveyed information to students to maximize their academic retention and achievement, I instead prioritized image, ego, and arrogance. And, from my vantage point, I was nowhere close to being the only teacher teaching in this context.

When teachers view the occupation as a verb rather than a noun, the true spirit of teaching is accomplished. When teaching becomes about how well the students learn rather than how well a teacher teaches, the proper perspectives remain intact and student achievement skyrockets. This was one of my initial (and most significant) downfalls. I wanted teaching to be about me — to be a "great teacher" — and student achievement took a backseat to how I was viewed professionally and socially. Being the "great teacher" or the "cool teacher" mattered more than being the *effective* teacher. A fine line, perhaps; but sometimes the fine lines are the toughest to cross.

---

138   One of my colleagues once asked me, "How does it feel to be the most popular teacher at the biggest high school in the state?" I shrugged it off with a smile, but the truth is, I loved every minute of it.

139   Somewhat reminiscent of when Apollo Creed told Rocky Balboa, "You fight great, but I'm a great fighter," after Rocky had defeated him, and Mr. T.

The Abstract Life

I taught English because it enabled me to implement "The Three Ls" of teaching English: Literature, Language, and Life. I loved being able to teach a novel and relate it to life, and I was always open about using my own personal experiences[140] as anecdotes to coincide with a particular "deeper perspective" displayed in whatever literary work I was teaching at the time. Admittedly, I enjoyed taking the works of writers like Kurt Vonnegut, William Golding, and Edith Wharton and applying them to relevant aspects of life. And as a contemporary teacher I feel that this was a paramount responsibility.

However, there is a very well-defined line that should not be crossed when it comes to teaching the aspect of life to students. As long as we were talking about life *in the abstract*, propriety remained intact. Contemporary students often need multiple perspectives on life lessons because many do not receive adequate guidance anywhere else. So teaching life lessons in the abstract, casting a wide net, is not only moral, legal, but imperative.

Teachers do their students a disservice if the only teach the content without relating it to how it can be applied in life, as long as they are teaching life in the abstract, not being specific to any particular student or including any details which would provide an inappropriately deep purview into a teacher's personal life. Therefore, painting a picture of life in broad strokes is more beneficial because it allows students to individually apply lessons to their lives when they may fit their own personal situations. However, it is incumbent upon the teacher to teach these lessons clearly, and it is incumbent upon the student to apply these lessons individually.

The Individual Life

Schools have counselors for a reason. When a student approaches a teacher to confide information about their personal struggles, family struggles, relationship struggles, substance abuse struggles, etc., it

---

140 This too perhaps pushed the limits of teacher propriety.

is the responsibility of the teacher to refer that student to a school counselor.

School counselors are one of the most under-used resources in education. Many (if not most) were once teachers themselves and understand the day-to-day grind of being a teacher. But their additional training and schooling in counseling is invaluable to the educational community because they are paid to provide the extra support to students beyond academics — teachers are not.

Giving personal advice to a student regarding non-academic issues is a very slippery slope, mainly for one specific reason: If a teacher gives a student a piece of advice, and that student acts upon the advice, the teacher is subsequently liable for the results of that advice or guidance if/when the result is unfavorable or damaging. So when a student seeks a teacher's advice regarding family or drugs or drinking or sex, it is not the teacher's place to have a heart-to-heart with the student. It may feel good to know a student trusts and values a teacher enough to want to confide deeply-personal details and information, but the simple fact of the matter is that the school counselors are the ones who are qualified and paid to deal with these student issues, not the teachers.

Even when the advice is good advice, it can still backfire. For example, a female student approached me and wanted to talk one-on-one because her boyfriend was pressuring her to have sex although she'd never had sex before. She talked about how he pushed the limits often and although she told him repeatedly she was not ready to enter into a physical relationship, he continued his persistence.

"Don't do it," I told her. "Once you've done it, there's no going back. I wish I'd waited."

So, this female student came to me and confided in me that her boyfriend wanted to have sex and my advice to her was to *not* have sex with him. However, at my sentencing hearing, the prosecutor made a factual (but misleading) statement, saying, "During our investigation, we learned that Mr. Brundage was having one-on-one conversations with female students about sex." Technically, this was true; the fact that I was telling her *not* to have sex did not seem to matter. Thus, even this was considered inappropriate.

Here's the thing: When these conversations begin, and physical intimacy becomes a topic of conversation between a student and teacher, there is often an unseen line being crossed. Allowing sex to be a topic of conversation can somehow also open it up as a viable option (whether this notion is acknowledged or not). Initially, this may seem completely unreasonable, but increasing statistics of unlawful teacher-student relationships would beg to differ.

There is nothing wrong with teaching *life*, as long as it is taught in the abstract. Having deep discussions about the intricacies of an individual student's life struggles is beyond teachers' scope of responsibility. Any topic which applies to a one-on-one situation with a student must be referred to the school counselor. With many topics, if a student confides something (such as abuse or neglect) to a teacher, and the teacher does not immediately report this information, he/she not only becomes open to liability, but could rightfully be fired for not disclosing information regarding the safety of a student. Moreover, if a student is discussing his/her sex life, it crosses a boundary as well. I told a student not to have sex with her boyfriend, advice which I believe was correct and sound advice. However, my error was in the simple fact that I should not have broached the topic of sex with her, *at all.*

My one-on-one conversations with Taissa ended up being a significant catalyst of our unlawful relationship. We talked about her sex life quite often.

CHAPTER THIRTEEN

When asked in an interview about relationships between female teachers and male students, Donald Trump told *Extra* in 2012 (at the Miss USA pageant, no less), "Well, I don't think the male students have been hurt by it. In fact, they're going around bragging about it as I understand it — I don't see a lot of damage done." This perspective (and errant assumption) is not a rare opinion. There is a perception among many people that there is no damage being done if these relationships are "consensual," especially regarding male students and female teachers. But the truth is evident: There *is* damage being done — to students of both genders.

Lasting Impact

Education Week interviewed a man named Jeff who was willing to speak candidly about the affair he had as a student with his adult female teacher. "Hollywood, they think it's such a hot thing when a guy gets laid at a young age. I tell you, it's not a hot thing," he told the online journal in 2007. "They say, 'That guy's lucky.' I say, no, he's not lucky at all."

The affair with his teacher lasted several months before his parents found out about it and pressured the teacher to resign from her position. As an adult, Jeff admitted he was left "with no boundaries" and has lived a life plagued by gambling, extra-marital affairs, and numerous ruined marriages, all of which he traces back to his affair with his teacher.

Education Week also interviewed Richard Gartner, a psychologist and author who published a book in 2005 about the lasting impact of sexual abuse. According to Mr. Gartner, victims of sexual abuse — whether or not it is perceived as "consensual" at the time — often struggle as adults with addictive behavior, compulsive disorders, and substance abuse; and their relationships as adults are often framed in the contexts of power and/or control rather than love and affection. And in many cases, the impacts of the abuse may not become fully apparent until they are 30-years-old or even later.

It haunts me daily that I may have had this sort of impact on someone. It haunts me daily that I have caused someone this sort of pain, because I know that pain all-too-well myself. There is nothing I can do now to ease the tragic and lasting impacts I may have had on Taissa's life. Much of the guilt I've been carrying through the years is centered on the incontrovertible fact that I may have damaged someone, for life. Yet, that never once occurred to me in the moments leading-up to our first kiss, and it should have. I should have known that I was about to cause a lasting and immeasurable amount of pain and damage. But I refused to see beyond my own personal errant logic and cognitive distortions.

"Pain is the only human process that is completely defined by the person experiencing it."[141]

Pain

For years, I kept the fact that I was sexually assaulted as a teenager buried as a deep dark secret – a *very* deep, *very* dark secret. It's

---

141 This quote, from the show *Scandal*, is pretty much the most perfect definition of "pain" I've ever heard, and it rings true in the most personal of ways.

humiliating to be a man, and a victim of rape. But I am, and nothing will ever change that.

I was raped.

I can say this now — "I was raped" — but until my offender treatment program during prison in Lansing, I'd never ever spoken audibly about my assault — *ever*. It was the gap in the plot; it was the hole in the storyline. I kept it a secret from everyone and buried it so deep, it almost began to seem like a bad dream — a nightmare — that never actually happened. But it did. It happened, and I never told anyone.

As a part of the treatment program in Lansing, we were required to write (and read aloud) our "autobiography"[142] to the treatment group. The group was comprised of twelve guys who were in prison for sex offenses, and of the twelve, eight were there because they did something to a relative; only four of us were there for a non-relative, and my former student was the oldest of anyone's victim, by several years.[143]

As each person read and presented their "autobiography," many of them told their own stories of being abused or assaulted, but I kept mine to myself. When I read my personal story aloud, I was brutally honest about everything I'd done — except *that*. And when I received feedback from the therapist, she flat-out called me on it.

"Something's missing," she said to me in front of the group. "No one just becomes what you were. Something's missing."

And, of course, I lied, saying something like, "No, that's everything."

She merely shook her head and sighed.

A few weeks later, I knew I needed to tell her. I went into her office after our group session one day, and I told her everything.

---

142 Essentially, this was our "life story" relating to how we became the monsters we'd become.

143 The treatment groups were divided by "theme," more-or-less. For example, there were no Internet crimes or violent crimes in our group; the "theme" for my group related to positions of authority.

I told her about how one night, the summer after I graduated from high school, my buddies and I went out drinking at a club in Wichita's *Old Town* called "The Cowboy" — a club which was extremely casual about asking for the proper ID before administering alcoholic beverages to patrons. We drank and danced and whatnot until the club closed, then we all went back to my house. I drank exceedingly more than usual that night, so going back to my house was my convenient preference.

After hanging out for an hour or so, my buddies decided it was time to call it a night, and they all left, except one. And this is where my memory of that night gets even more hazy. I was excessively drunk; I was sitting on my bed leaning against the headboard, trying not to throw-up, and I was reasonably certain that I was ready to slip into a drunken coma(ish) slumber. But since one remaining friend was still lingering there — lurking in the drunken fog of my peripheral vision — I felt the social (and obligatory) responsibility to remain awake as his host. I cannot recall what he was saying as he began rambling along with (what sounded like) a heart-felt soliloquy about one thing or another, but I remember him getting up from his chair and slithering across my bedroom to sit down next to me on my bed.

My memory of this point in the night is more like flashes or film clips, like an old 8-millimeter reel-to-reel home movie being projected onto a grayish wall; no sound, and numerous frames cut out and haphazardly taped back together, clicking and clacking sloppily through an old movie projector.

I felt paralyzed. I felt that if I moved, I would throw up; and even though my body remained motionless, the room sluggishly swayed like a rickety old sailboat in the wilderness of a wavy dark open sea. It was as though I was powerless and completely at the mercy of what would happen next.

And then, what happened next, did.

I refuse to put the details of my assault into print, but that night, unable to move, unable to speak, unable to think — it happened.

I was raped.

"And that, Mr. Brundage, is the missing piece," the therapist said to me in Lansing during our one-on-one conversation.

I had no reply to this.

"Don't you see?" she asked me. "You talked in your Autobiography about how all of your out-of-control sexual behavior started in college and as a young adult, but you never mentioned what could have started it." She looked to me for a reaction, but I was statuesque — motionless.

"Hmm," I replied, monosyllabically.

"It makes perfect sense," she said with an air of optimism, feeling as though we'd had the quintessential *breakthrough.* "Your promiscuous behavior in college and as a young adult was your own subconscious way of trying to regain control of your own sexuality;" she paused, "and prove to yourself that you weren't gay."

The moment she dropped this on me, I suddenly felt like I had to look back and redefine my entire life. I'd lived with this pain, buried so deep for so long, and now that I'd actually spoken about it — audibly, using consonants and vowels and nouns and verbs and punctuation — suddenly, it was real.

And I wept.

That night, I told my wife, in a letter. I couldn't stand the thought of telling her something else that might make her think differently of me, so I wrote it. After all, writing is what I do, and that was the best way I could imagine telling her. And a few days later, when she received the letter, she reaffirmed that this revelation did not diminish the way she thought of me. We talked about it in-person at her next visit, and since then, we've moved forward.

During a follow-up one-on-one conversation with the therapist the following week, we spoke about how I was dealing with the fact that people now knew. I told her that it still didn't really feel real — it was essentially "horrifyingly surreal," as I put it — so she instructed me to do one thing.

"Repeat after me," she said. "Say, *I was raped.*" I looked at her, bewildered and dumbfounded. *Absolutely not*, I thought to myself. But she just stared at me.

"Go ahead," she said, "say it."

And I could tell from the way in which she intently locked her sights on me that I wasn't going to walk out of that room until I'd complied. And yet, I remained mute.

The silence in the room was deafening. I could hear my heart pounding against its better judgment. I could feel my teeth grinding like an unstable submerged ocean fault line, ready to slip and set-off a tsunami of emotion. And still, she stared. So, with seemingly no other option, my vocal cords primed for use and I inhaled, knowing that when the oxygen currently rushing into my lungs subsequently rushed out as carbon-dioxide, that air would form words, and those words would say something I'd never said before, but had known, for sixteen years, was true.

"I was raped," I said. The quiver in my voice was audibly visible.

The words sounded hesitant, uneasy, afraid to step into the open air, like James Spader as he nervously stepped into the *Stargate* for the first time. Those three syllables shattered the silence like an assassin's bullet. Those three words seemed to somehow speak the past into existence.

Days earlier, I'd described in detail (as much as my tattered memory would provide) what had been done to me that night in 1998, but it didn't seem real; as though it hadn't happened to me, but rather to the protagonist of a book I'd written. But when I heard my own voice say, "I was raped," it was suddenly *very* real.

And it hurt.

I remember crying, again, uncontrollably; and rather than saying anything to me, the therapist let me get it out of my system and allowed me to regain my composure before continuing our conversation.

Here's where it gets stranger: When I stood up to leave that session with the therapist, I literally felt lighter. I felt like I was suddenly and simultaneously stronger and slimmer, as though I'd sat down wearing a suit of armor, but stood up wearing silk pajamas. And ever since that day, that event — the 1998 assault on my body, my masculinity, my self-image, and my soul — holds no power over me. So now, I can talk about being a victim of rape. I can talk openly about it with the confidence of knowing I survived a sexual assault.

I don't blame my past sexual behavior or my crime on being raped. It was, of course, a catalyst to my slow-growing addiction to sex, but I had a choice — I always had a choice. I wasn't an adulterous womanizing criminal because I was raped. But I do understand this: Of the many contributing factors, that one was the most significant.

"You're a classic case of the *Cycle of Abuse*," the therapist told me in our final one-on-one session. That very well may be. And if so, it is my responsibility to do everything in my power to halt that cycle with every fiber of my being.

Insight

This is the insight I lacked when I had the relationship with my former student. I existed in a very dangerous contextual cacophony of ignorance, arrogance, and depression. And now that I'm aware of a significant root cause of this, it pains me to know that I've caused the same pain in someone else.

Sexual misconduct carries a seemingly-endless ripple effect throughout the entire lives of those who have been forced to suffer through it. Assuming a student is "okay" with having a relationship with a teacher is like saying I was okay with what that guy did to me because I was drunk. Any teacher who considers a relationship with a student to be permissible is only setting that student up for a lifetime of difficulties with future relationships, submitting to authority, self-esteem, self-worth, and even substance abuse and/or depression.

The only thing more painful than the impact of my own sexual assault was knowing I have caused this same lasting pain to someone else. She will never forgive me, and I will never forgive myself.

CHAPTER FOURTEEN

The issue of inappropriate teacher-student relationships is not going to simply vanish on its own, and current efforts to eradicate the epidemic from the educational system have failed. The problem persists because there are more variables and contributing factors than anyone wants to admit or address. And the problem is serious enough that a new and larger approach is warranted.

Bigger in Texas

Exactly how big of a problem is this? To answer that question, one needs only to look at the great state of Texas. According to CBS News in 2016, Texas was well on-track to breaking its own record for illegal teacher-student relationships. Between September 1, 2014 and May 31, 2015 (essentially, one school year), the Texas Education Agency investigated an alarming 162 instances of inappropriate teacher-student relationships. In that same time frame one year later, the number rose to 188, which was the fifth consecutive annual increase. This number is at least calculable; the incalculable number is the illegal teacher-student relationships which go unreported, undetected, and unpunished.

Texas even went as far as holding hearings before a state legislative panel regarding this issue. Among those who testified at these hearings was the director of the Children's Advocacy Centers of Texas, Christina Green. She was very forward and blunt about the issue, stating, "Our goal, outside of preventing these inappropriate relationships from ever developing, should be to identify and quash these cases at the point of grooming before any abuse happens." She went on to say in her testimony that schools tend to pretend the issue simply does not exist because it's a difficult topic to bring up with the faculty.

Ms. Green made a solid point with her observation. Teachers are smart people, but the problem with bringing up this issue in the forward manner in which it needs to be approached is the risk of offending and/or alienating the faculty. A principal or in-service presenter who broaches this topic in a faculty meeting may evoke negative reactions and his/her point would likely be lost. Teachers who have relationships with students are certainly in the minority. But teachers acquainted with a teacher who is having a relationship with a student are in a massive majority (whether they are aware of it or not). Awareness of this issue for teachers goes beyond simply saying, "Don't have an inappropriate relationship;" it is equally important to educate teachers on the signs and indicators that a colleague may be engaging in such a relationship or is predicating such a situation.

I somewhat disagree with Ms. Green regarding the "grooming" issue. While some teachers who cross this line do "groom" a student for a relationship, I think far fewer teachers actually seek-out a student with whom they can interact inappropriately. These predatory "grooming" teachers do exist — there's no denying that. But the far more common instances which lead to the inappropriate relationships have less to do with the proactive process of the adult grooming the student and more to do with the adult simply distorting his/her own reality so far that the student is viewed as a peer rather than a product of the work environment. And this, in my opinion, is an even bigger and more dangerous problem than grooming. Grooming is intentional — even predatory. However, the errant cognitive re-categorization of seeing students as peers happens over time as a result of becoming too comfortable and inappropriately familiar with students based on non-sexual motives. These motives then grow beyond propriety.

Research

This perspective is supported by research, going all the way back to 1995 in a four-year study by Charol Shakeshaft, formerly of Hofstra University, currently of Virginia Commonwealth University. The study, appearing in the education journal *Phi Delta Kappan* in March of 1995, stated specifically, "These abusers saw their actions as either harmless or romantic." She refers to these instances in her study as "bad judgment romances." Shakeshaft told the *New York Times*, the "bad judgment abusers outnumbered pedophiles — who seek work in schools to molest children — 2 to 1."

Shakeshaft's study also indicated female students who had relationships with teachers "most often looked mature for their age and had 'bad girl' reputations." This *does not* mean the relationship is her fault — at all. However, when it comes to teachers' cognitive distortions and re-categorizing students as peers (or even seeing them as adults) rather than students, observing someone who "appears" or "acts" more "mature" can contribute to these tragic and deluded cognitive distortions. But the fact is simple: Just because a student "looks" or "acts" mature does not make him/her open to (or capable of) an adult relationship.[144]

Unfortunately, there *are* teachers who specifically seek students for sex. These are predators who need to be locked away. But according to Shakeshaft's study, the majority of teachers who have relationships with students did not intentionally seek out the situation from the beginning; the situation festered from a long series of borderline

---

144 Actually, simply being a student at all makes them completely off-limits, but stating this obvious fact has had little-to-no impact on the situation.

choices and tragic cognitive distortions. This, of course, *does not* alleviate their responsibility for their actions — they are still guilty, *as was I* — but what this *does* do is change the manner in which school districts and school officials should be addressing this issue, both proactively and preventatively.

CHAPTER FIFTEEN

There have been several glimmers of hope. Holding those accountable for their direct action is important, but holding those accountable for their indirect (or lack of) action is equally as vital. Teachers who cross the lines of propriety with students should be prosecuted to the fullest extent of the law. However, school administrators and district officials who blatantly overlook or cover-up these instances must be held equally accountable.

Accountability

In 2016, a teacher in La Cygne, Kansas was arrested and charged with having sex with several of his students. And while this teacher, Keaton Krell, was facing 20 counts of unlawful sexual misconduct, sitting in jail under a $200,000 bond, the district superintendent, Chris Kleidotsy, suddenly decided to take a superintendent job in a different school district in Kansas. This may not have seemed odd at the time, but in 2017 he too faced charges, along with the principal of the school where the sexual misconduct occurred, Tim Weis. However, they were not charged with sexual misconduct; they were charged with failing to report child abuse. The principal and superintendent knew about this teacher's actions, and did nothing — they covered it up. And when this became a fact which could no longer be ignored, the justice system took the necessary steps to hold them accountable for their actions (or lack thereof) as well.

This is not the norm, but it is a step in the right direction. The general public sees when teachers are arrested, charged, and jailed for their sexual misconduct with students; yet what remains unseen is the alarming number of school and district administrators who were (or are) aware of these ongoing instances, but fight to keep them out of the public eye.

But why would school and district officials — many (or most) of whom were teachers at one point — choose to hide these crimes?

Across the country, high schools and colleges are facing countless lawsuits based on the sexual misconduct of faculty and staff members, and as a result, school reputations are being scarred, administrators are being fired, and money is being paid-out by the millions. Thus, in order to avoid further humiliation, lawsuits, and loss of high-level jobs, many districts (including the district where I was teaching when I committed my crimes) have taken to handling these issues "internally" when possible.

So here is how it works: When a teacher-student relationship is discovered, there are typically two ways the "discovery" happens. Either the parents go to the police first, and the police inform the school (and district), and the teacher is arrested (which is what happened in my case); *or* the parents go to the school first, the school informs the district, and the police are never contacted — the matter is handled "internally." When the parents go to the police first, these are the instances which typically garner media attention.

Hush-Hush

The tragic fact of this sequence of events is this: When the school is contacted first and the police are not informed, it becomes *hush-hush*. In fact, it happens enough that the people in the upper-level district administrative offices and the Human Resources department of my former district all had a "code term" for this — when another teacher is caught having another relationship with another student (most often at one of the high schools), district administrators merely say amongst themselves that they "have to buy another Cadillac," which is their casual and cryptic nomenclature for providing a "satisfactory resolution" for the family of a student who had a relationship with a teacher. Subsequently, the teacher is sometimes "transferred" or "resigns for health reasons" or takes an "early retirement" (the "early retirement" one actually happened at my school while I was teaching there), or some other excuse to keep things under wraps. The most ridiculous excuse I heard was when a "staff member" was forced to suddenly resign because of something he'd posted on Facebook — and the administration actually expected people to believe that. However, in all seriousness, if the voters knew how many high school teachers were having sex with students, school board turnover would hit a record-high.

Unfortunately, school districts have been "buying Cadillacs" for decades — and it's wrong. The parents of my former student were absolutely right for going to the police rather than going to the school or the district. If a teacher is having a relationship with a student, it is a matter for the law to handle, not the Human Resources department of the school district. There are teachers at nearly every school who have had relationships with students, and those students have long-since graduated, so those teachers have essentially "gotten away with it" and will never be punished. And with many of these relationships, the school administrators knew (or at least suspected) something was going on.

They Knew

I am nearly certain the administrators at my school knew about me as well (perhaps not the specifics, but they knew). As a teacher at that school, I had the privilege of teaching at the high school from which I graduated, and I was extremely popular with the faculty as well as the students and parents. But suddenly, one day, I walked into the principal's office with my letter of resignation, announcing that I was taking a teaching job in a small town for less money, far away. There was an understanding there; he knew why I was leaving and I knew why I was leaving. My wife and I made the decision months earlier after I'd confessed everything to her, and when I announced that I was leaving, I was given the old "Okay, good luck;" and that was it. I would bet my bottom dollar that he knew good-and-well why I was leaving, and he was simply glad that I was moving on, not to be his problem anymore.

About a month before I was arrested and my relationship with the student hit the news, my (former) best friend (who is now my Archenemy) and I went to the winter Homecoming basketball game — as an alumnus, not a former faculty member. I strolled around and said "Hi" to some of my former co-workers, including the "Okay, good luck" principal as well as a few of the assistant principals. The head principal greeted me with a smile and happily shook my hand and asked me how I was doing — all-the-while knowing what I'd done because the police had already informed him of the allegations (and I doubt they expected me to show up on campus).

I remember my exchange with him specifically, but I also remember one other exchange with one of the assistant principals very vividly. She was at the basketball game in a supervisory role and when I walked up and said "Hi" to her, she didn't seem happy to see me at all. She wasn't rude, but her demeanor toward me could be sufficiently described as "civilly cold" (and I picked up on it immediately). In previous years, during my administrative internship at the school, she was the assistant principal with whom I'd worked the most (and who'd taught me the most about being an administrator) so I was very happy to see her. But when she wouldn't even make eye-contact with me, I knew something was wrong — and on a deep level, I knew exactly what that *something* was.

Somehow, I knew she knew. But here's the thing: I respect her so much more for being cold toward me than I do the "Okay, good luck" principal for being bogus and fake and falsely happy to see me. The assistant principal knew how she felt, and I'm certain she wasn't at all allowed to talk to me about it (obviously), but the fact that she didn't give me a fake sense of politeness actually makes me respect her so much more. And if she would ever speak to me again (which I doubt, understandably), I would thank her for that.

CHAPTER SIXTEEN

I t is exceedingly easier to point an accusatory finger at the television when another teacher-student relationship is aired and say things like "pervert" or "sick" or "pedophile" or any number of related barbs. It is the easiest explanation for the epidemic and it allows humans to set themselves apart from those who partake in actions of which they disapprove. But in a vast majority of cases, these assumptions — these barbs — are not accurate.

Shadenfreude

"Shadenfreude. From the German words, Schaden and Freude, *damage* and *joy*. It means to take spiteful, malicious delight in the misfortune of others. We used to dismiss this as simply an ugly side of human nature, but it is much, *much* more than that. Recently a Stanford professor actually captured Schadenfreude on a brain scan. It's a physiological medical phenomenon. When we see others fall it sometimes causes a chemical to be released in the dorsal striatum of the brain which actually causes us to feel pleasure."

-James Spader

(as Alan Shore on *Boston Legal*)

When a teacher has an inappropriate relationship with a student, the knee-jerk assumption is to accuse the teacher of being a sick-in-the-head sexual predator who preys upon high school students. This is not considered an unreasonable assumption and it certainly is not an uncommon assumption either. And considering the level of Shadenfreude which regularly marinates in America's 24-hour news cycle, it is not an unreasonable conclusion. We like seeing people go down in flames. We like seeing people fail; we *love* seeing people fail, because seeing someone else fail is just as good as succeeding ourselves, simply because we have been conditioned to see the failures of others as our non-failures, and we perceive those non-failures as victories when, in reality, those things have nothing to do with our own lives.

Vengeance

It is a form of surrogate vengeance. And we want our vengeance. We *need* our vengeance. We take comfort in our vengeance. As contemporary hype-driven consumers, we want (and need) those opportunities to see someone else writhing in self-imposed despotism, just to be able to say, "See, look at that horrible person. I'm nothing like that person — that person is not me."

> "Vengeance is something that society needs from time to time — if for no other purpose, then to keep the rest of us sane. —— Vengeance keeps us sane. What a fascinating statement!"
>
> -Jason Alexander
>
> (as Professor Rothchild on *Criminal Minds*)

I was asked about this in an interview once, regarding why people seem to enjoy are so vengeful in their reactions (specifically Internet comments) regarding issues like mine and others, and my response was, "It is so much easier to reference teachers who have made these choices as 'sick,' 'pedophile,' 'weird,' 'perverted,' — it's easy to point fingers and use malicious words." The public needs to find a way to belittle, ridicule, and demean those who make choices which are perceived as violating social norms, laws, and traditions. But the key is, it makes people literally feel better to do that because as long as there is someone in the line of fire of the stones they are casting, no one is casting stones at them.

But what if — just what if — the public viewed people with the perspective of, "Why did this person make that choice, and how can we make them a better person as a result?" Granted, that just sounds like altruistic nonsense, like something Jesus would say.

Help a bad person become a good person? Nonsense. We *need* bad people to stay bad so that we can maintain our own perceived sense of goodness and superiority. Besides, if a bad person can become good, then inversely, a good person can become bad. And we all think we're "good people" and we refuse to acknowledge our own human capacity for evil, regardless of the size, scope, or significance.

I guarantee, if we take a deep look into the lives of teachers who have had relationships with students, we will find a heartbreaking list of instances of their own victimizations, assault, abuse, and/or neglect. So as humans, we need to help and love those who have suffered through these tragedies, regardless of whether or not these tragedies have led to their own abusive behaviors. Crime must be punished, of course — but pain must be healed.

But it is far easier to hate than it is to love.

Take My Word For It

People hate me — *a lot.* It is an understandable assumption that I am a horrible human being. After all, my name appears on the most shameful "list" known to man. I am a criminal. I am a felon. For the rest of my life, I will have a criminal record. For the rest of my life, I will have a Department of Corrections ID Number (#104403, in case you were wondering). For many (if not most) people, who I *was* is who I shall *always be*. Who I am *now* seems irrelevant when seen in the shadow of who I was.

How many years did I spend, living the life of a selfish cheating liar? Too many. I spent the first five years of my marriage caring only for myself and taking my wife for granted. On top of that, I hurt numerous people along the way. Anything I did, I did for me.

As a result, I'm reasonably certain there's a deep dark room in Hell reserved just for me.

One day, a few years after my release from prison, I called the hotline for RAINN (Rape, Abuse, & Incest National Network). I guess I'd just reached a point that I needed to talk about being raped. I talked about it in prison, and I've spoken to a local therapist briefly about it, but my biggest question lingered: Should I report my rape?

I dialed the hotline number, dialing *67 on my iPhone before dialing the number (to hide my caller ID, though I'm really not sure why), and the hotline began to ring. I pressed 1, as prompted by the menu and was transferred to another ringing line. This line rang approximately seven times, but as it rang, talking about my rape again became more real, so I pressed the red hang-up button on my phone and sat it down on the table in front of me. I stared-off for several minutes, as though my iPhone was an open window into the outside world — a world of people who would peek in and ridicule my assault. "You're a guy who was raped by a guy?" they would say with laughter. I just knew they would.

I hold a deep respect for the strength it took for my former student to step forward and reveal our relationship. She is a much stronger person than I, because I can't bring myself to tell the police I was raped.

By the way, in case you were wondering, there is no statute of limitations on rape — and with the way I struggle with it, I completely understand why. I could literally walk into a police station right now and report it. But I'm not.

In one of my interviews with the media, I told the reporter that I was fully aware of numerous instances of other teachers at my former school who either had or were having relationships with students. She asked me why I didn't speak up now and turn them in. Valid question. I told her about my rape, but I told her I also couldn't bring myself to put anyone through the devastating life destruction I experienced, whether they deserved it or not. I suppose that's why I haven't reported my rapist, so that is probably also why I have not reported these other teachers. Besides, in the legal community, I have zero credibility, so no one would believe me anyway. But even with that, if I can't bring myself to report my own rapist, I certainly can't report someone else's. Admittedly, this is a serious flaw with me, and hopefully, someday, it will change. Maybe someday I will. I can only hope.

The only people who know the identity of my rapist are my wife and my little sister. But lots of teachers at my former school are aware of which teachers are having relationships with students — it's part of that *hush-hush* subculture, the after 3PM underworld which formulates in secret, shadowed by dark hallways and locked doors. It's the worst kept secret in the educational community, which is why I get frustrated when the public and school officials are "outraged" every other week when another teacher is arrested.

Is anyone "outraged" that I was raped? I doubt it. People probably think I deserved it (regardless of the fact that it happened in the summer of 1998). Reporting my rape would only ruin someone else's life; it wouldn't make my life any better — in fact, I'd probably feel guilty for causing someone else's life to crumble, even though he violated me in the worst conceivable way.

I want to create, not destroy. That's why I write, that's why I give speeches, that's why I'm an activist against unlawful teacher-student relationships. I want to help stop sexual assaults before they happen. However, in the wake of the assaults that have already occurred, there is a battle within myself regarding what to do, how to feel, and how to act.

My whole life is about moving forward. If I report my rapist, I am merely dwelling on the past, trying to alter something that will never change.

That being said, if someone else reported it, I would cooperate fully. A fine line, I suppose, but I've clearly given up on trying to figure myself out.

I was raped. That will never change, regardless of whether he is punished or not.

Fact.

But here's my point: People prefer to continue to hurl malicious words at me, regardless of the efforts I currently make to combat the issue of unlawful teacher-student relationships. And these same people find it easier to call me a sick perverted pedophile than to offer a word of consolation to me as a sexual assault victim.

I am a rape survivor, but people would rather hurl insults because of my crime than offer love and kindness to a rape victim.

That's just how people are.

Fact.

I Get It.

In reading some Internet comments about me after prison as the media has covered my book and my speaking engagements, I've seen numerous comments from people I once knew (but with whom I haven't interacted in years). Some of them are people I knew in high school, but most are former students, most of whom I had a positive rapport (or even friendship) with me before my crime. And now, they are some of my most vocal opponents.

I wish I could say that I didn't understand why this was, but I totally get it. They feel (understandably) betrayed — specifically my former students. They, at one point, had significant respect for me as one of their teachers, only to see me on the news, violating my profession in the worst possible way. I did nothing to them specifically, but since I did something reprehensible, I violated their trust. And their gut-reaction is to loathe me with every fiber of their being. So I get it. I completely get it.

My loudest opponent is a former student who took my class during my fifth year of teaching.[145] She has unleashed numerous Twitter diatribes about me, my favorite being the simple (but to-the-point) Tweet: "Kurt Brundage is human garbage." The crazy thing is, when she was in my class, she always insisted on the front row, we had a very positive (and appropriate) rapport, and on the last day of school, her class gave me a surprise group-hug and someone took a picture of it — a picture I still have. So, I didn't directly do anything to her which spawned this hatred; this vengeance is spawned by the fact that I committed the crime I committed. But, again, I get it. But what she (and most others) don't understand is this: They hate a person who no longer exists.

It's a convoluted triangle of misperception. Back then, she thought I was a good person, although I was (secretly) a terrible person. Then, she became aware of the terrible things I did, and in her mind, I was a terrible person. Now, she hates me because she thinks I'm a terrible person, even though I am now (with the help of therapy and especially my wife) the best kind of person I've ever been. Essentially, if you take all her slanderous words and apply them to who I was in 2010, she would be absolutely correct — but she's referencing an individual who no longer exists. I'm proud to not be that "human garbage" anymore, but the problem is, no one wants to see that. No one wants to see the change, they only want to embrace the evil of the past, regardless of the good that exists in the present.

It is far easier to hate than it is to love.

---

145 ...and she'll love the fact that I'm mentioning her in this book. [insert sarcastic voice]

CHAPTER SEVENTEEN

There is a categorical inequality lingering within the crevices of this issue. The perceptive nature of crimes involving sex between a teacher and a student should be absolute, but it is merely subjective. And this subjectivity hangs on one variable: Gender. It has always been interesting (in a sadly pathetic sort of way) to read Internet comments on stories about teachers who have been arrested for having a relationship with a student.

Backlash: Male

When my crime became public, the local media covered it with all the diligence of a medium-size city searching fervently for the latest scandal to air. Teacher-student scandals fill a convenient niche for local media outlets because they carry the variables of scandal, outrage, sex, and secrets — and sadly, the viewing public just eats that up. So upon hitting the airwaves and the Internet, I followed the public reaction to my downfall by reading the user comments on Facebook and the local news websites. And they were none-too-pleasant. Words like "sicko" and "pedophile" were the mildest comments. Statements such as, "Get a rope," or "Hang him on the school house lawn," or "All we need is one bullet" carried the general sentiment of the public toward me. Granted, I am not saying I did not deserve this reaction from the public (whose trust I'd clearly betrayed), but it illustrates the initial foundation of the public's perceptive inequality on this issue regarding gender. When the teacher is male, the public perceives him as a sick twisted pedophile who should be promptly executed.

Backlash: Female

When the teacher is a woman, the sentiment carries an entirely different theme. Suddenly, the Internet comments become, "Lucky kid!" or "Where were these teachers when I was in school?" or "She was just teaching him sex education;" and invariably, someone almost always posts some (or all) of the lyrics from Van Halen's "Hot for Teacher." It's as though people actually enjoy hearing about the conquests of a teenage boy who manages to hook-up with his attractive female teacher. The online journal *Education Week* summed it up sufficiently by saying, "They are crimes and abuses, but often they're treated as entertainment."

In Utah, 35-year-old Brianne Altice, an attractive blonde teacher, was arrested for having a sexual relationship with a teenage student. Then, while out on bail for that crime, she was arrested *again*! As the Fox affiliate in Salt Lake City reported, "the new alleged sexual offenses with an underage teen boy happened while 35-year-old Brianne Altice was out on bail awaiting trial for previous felony sex charges." So, this woman was a repeat-offender — even after being arrested — and yet, she is still not viewed by the public as being a "pedophile" or "pervert" or "predator." Here are the comments left on the news website regarding this teacher:

- "I wish I would've had teachers like these. Nothing wrong with it, guys were old enough to know what was going on. I doubt any of them lost their virginities to her… Although it's wrong to have done it on school property, I don't see anything wrong with it happening out of school. Everyone needs some fun."

- "She is cute, I would have hit that in high school."
- "One man's trash is another man's treasure. Wish I had teachers like this in high school."
- "I doubt they were held at knife point and raped. I doubt she forced them to undress."
- Interestingly, one comment bravely stated, "Reverse the genders and think about it again." Yet, before the gravity of this enlightenment could be grasped, someone else replied, "Well of course it's not right the other way around. Come on now…" Thus, not only does the hypocritical double-standard exists, it is seemingly acknowledged and condoned. Therefore, as long as the student is male and the teacher is female and (at least somewhat) attractive, the public scrutiny is not wholly negative.

A quick Google search reveals pages entitled, "20 Hot Teachers That Slept With Their Students"[146] and "10 Hottest Teachers Caught Sleeping With Their Students" — all women. MTV saw fit to publish an article on their website entitled "Two Female Teachers Arrested for Threesome with Male Student" — but the article centered more on the student bragging about his escapade rather than the crime itself; MTV, however, was sure to cover their ethical bases by including a quote from the local police chief who said, "No matter what sex the victim is, everyone should be outraged."

In 2002, a 43-year-old female teacher was arrested and charged with having sex with one of her students. The judge, Superior Court Judge Bruce A. Gaeta, sentenced her to probation — even after she'd agreed to a three-year prison term — justifying his judicial decision by saying, "It's just something between two people that clicked beyond the teacher-student relationship." The student was 13-years-old.

---

146 Granted, you can't put a whole lot of stock into people who haven't even mastered basic grammar. It should be "who," not "that."

A Disturbing Trend

I sat in a waiting room one day awaiting an appointment, scrolling through my iPhone for something to occupy my attention until my name was called. I opened a local news app and began reading the latest headlines, as I often do with the apps of the three local Wichita news stations. And as I scrolled down, I saw a headline that prompted me to click. The headline read, "Former Eureka teacher & coach pleads guilty in child sex crime case." Obviously this type of headline caught my eye, considering in 2012, a similar headline ran about me.

As the story stated, an attractive female teacher named Kourtnie Sanchez admitted to an inappropriate relationship with *three* high school boys. And the result of her sentencing hearing — her punishment for haphazardly inviting *three* high school boys into her sex life: *Probation.*

I was understandably frustrated with this because I was charged with having a relationship with *one* girl (which did not include sex); Sanchez was charged with having sex with *three* boys. I went to prison for two years, she received only eighteen months of probation. She received less probation than I received prison time.

Clearly, an issue of discrepancy exists.

I'm not saying I should have been given probation — I'm saying she should have gone to prison.

This trend is scary, but this trend is sickeningly normal. The website comments on these stories show the clear discrepancy. When a man commits these actions, he's a "sick" "twisted" "predator" "pedophile" and should be promptly executed on the school yard lawn (all of which was said about me). However, when a woman commits nearly identical crimes, suddenly it's the "lucky boy."

There is a well-known (yet seldom-remedied) inequality in the punitive measures taken against male teachers and female teachers when a relationship with a student occurs. When a female teacher is caught sending naked pictures like the ones Kourtnie Sanchez sent to numerous male students: Probation. Or if a female teacher is caught having a year-long sexual relationship with a student, as was the case with former Clearwater, Kansas teacher Cathleen Balman who, in May of 2013 admitted to having a full-on sexual intercourse relationship with a 15-year-old boy that lasted over a year: Probation. (For comparison's sake, the relationship with my former student lasted a mere four weeks, and we "made-out" only four times - we never had sex).

I'm not saying I should have been given probation — I'm saying they should have gone to prison.

We were teachers. We were mentors, leaders, role models — we were entrusted with the safety and security of these students and we violated that trust in the worst possible way. How can any parent trust the school system when teachers are taking advantage of students, school districts are sweeping instance-after-instance under the rug, and the judicial system (on which these parents depend for justice) selectively allows some teachers to simply walk away with probation?

The Balman case really does upset me, personally. This woman had a year-long sexual affair with this boy, exchanged *sext*-messages with him, and she'd even groomed him since being his junior high English teacher from several years prior. When it comes to logistical severity, her crime far exceeded mine. And here's another kicker: We both were prosecuted by the *same Sedgwick County Assistant District Attorney*. It blows my mind that he couldn't manage to send a woman — a teacher — to prison who admitted to *having repeated sex* with a 15-year-old boy, after having *me* sent to prison for *making-out* with a 15-year-old girl a few times (but then again, my sentencing hearing was on the Friday before the 2012 Election Day, the courtroom was full of television cameras, and my judge was running for re-election.

I'm not saying I should have been given probation — I'm saying she should have gone to prison.

Statistical Imbalance

A newspaper in New Jersey, *The New Jersey Star-Ledger*, did an investigative report about this issue. They found that male teachers do indeed received harsher sentences than female teachers who commit the same crime. In fact, the study examined nearly 100 cases and found that 54% of men received prison time and only 44% of women did, and the duration of those sentences differed as well, men getting an average sentence of nearly two-and-a-half years, while women averaged just over eighteen months. So clearly, an imbalance exists.

My prison sentence was appropriate. In fact, I probably deserved *more* time. The pain I've caused is unforgivable. I let more people down than I will ever truly know, and I carry that guilt with me daily. Anyone who was once a student of mine is now in college or beyond, and some still talk to me — many have forgiven me for my actions and accept (and hopefully appreciate) who I am now. And for that, I am exceedingly appreciative and grateful. I've made no secret of my struggles to live a better life, but here's the thing: *If I'd walked away with probation, the extent to which I have changed the very nucleus of my existence would have been to a far lesser degree.* I do not — at *all* — regret the time I spent in prison. I was living an out-of-control lifestyle and prison was exactly the punch in the face I needed. I have become the best possible version of myself because I was fully held accountable for my actions. And while I still have struggles, I am not even an afterthought of the human garbage I was in 2010 — *Thank God!*

Now, I live a life worth living rather than a life worth hiding. And if Judge Philip Journey had given me probation on that day, November 2, 2012, there's a good chance that I would never have come to the realization that I was as broken as I was — I may have never taken the time to fix the underlying problems which led to my tragic choices.

A teacher who has a relationship with a student needs to go to prison. I needed to go to prison. In comparison, the severity of Cathleen

Balman's crime exceeded mine; the quantity of Kourtnie Sanchez's crime exceeded mine. And yet, they both walked away with probation — this is the unfortunate rule, not the exception, for women. When the justice system applies lighter sentences to female teachers who have the same relationships that would send a male teacher to prison, the justice system fails. People must stop considering male students in these situations "lucky guys" while in the same breath calling the female students "victims." *They're all victims.* Stop making "Hot for Teacher" jokes about the female teachers while demanding that the male teachers be locked-up. We all deserve to be locked-up. Lord knows I did.

So as long as the *perceptions* of these crimes differ, so will the *punishments*. Cute blonde teachers like Kourtnie Sanchez will continue to sleep with students, get caught, get probation, and change nothing about their lives. And any female teacher seeing these sentences of probation being handed out left-and-right is going to be less likely to second-guess her actions if she's ever in a situation where an inappropriate relationship can take place. As far as she can tell, she'll just get probation and find a new job.

I'm not saying I should have been given probation - I'm saying they should go to prison.

All of them.

CHAPTER EIGHTEEN

The manner in which teachers view students in their own psyche has the greatest impact on how a teacher subsequently interacts with students during (or beyond) the school day. Thus, if a teacher's personal view of students is that of a work-product and intellectual molding, that is typically a safe mindset. However, when teachers view students as part of their social (or emotional) paradigm, the line-blurring begins, even if the teacher has neither said nor done anything inappropriate.

Mindset

It all comes down to mindset. The binding crux of proper and improper behavior by teachers is centered around mindset. When a teacher allows him/herself to step beyond the context of teacher, the blurring of lines begins. However, — *and this is important* — that particular *step* occurs more often in a teacher's mind than in a teacher's classroom. "It's all in the mind."[147]

---

147 …as George Harrison said in the 1968 film, *Yellow Submarine.*

In February of 2017, a video[148] surfaced of six teachers and a school secretary in Bangor, Michigan speaking socially about their students at a bar, playing a game apparently entitled "Marry, F--k, Kill"[149] where each of them can be clearly heard saying which students with whom they, among other things, would have sex. One male teacher can be heard saying he preferred a particular female student because "she's cool, and she never brought up that I was wasted on the bus trip; she can keep secrets." This sort of off-the-cuff insight comes only from someone who has previously contemplated the possibility of an inappropriate relationship with a student, even if no inappropriate behavior occurred.

And yet, his statement perfectly illustrates the overall point about mindset. This man engaged in previous inappropriate behavior (being "wasted" on a bus trip) and more-or-less got away with it, leading to his further pushing of limits. In his mind, his actions were permissible because no consequences were rendered, even though a *student* was aware of him being intoxicated during a school function.

At the Bangor school board meeting following the release of this video, parents packed the meeting, hoping to voice their concerns about the troubling behavior seen on this video, and asking why more action was not taken. And after given a brief opportunity to speak, the school board did nothing — *absolutely nothing*. They told the parents and citizens in the meeting that all appropriate steps had been taken and no further disciplinary actions were necessary. And once the comments ended, the board moved to a closed-door session and refused to talk to anyone else. However, after parents refused to leave, the school board eventually returned to the public meeting room, accompanied by an attorney retained by the school district. The attorney then fed the crowd a complete falsehood, saying,

---

148   This video can be readily found on YouTube.

149   (or something like that.) And granted, "kill" is disturbing as well, but that's a subject for a whole other book. Thus, while I am not ignoring or minimizing that particular aspect of their "game," the other parts are this book's focal points.

"You can't point to anywhere on that video where the teachers were talking about students."[150] This was clearly an outright lie since the teachers in the video were specifically using students' names. "It is false," the lawyer continued, "that any teachers here suggested any sexual activity with any students." Of course, anyone who viewed the unedited and uncensored video knew this statement to be completely untrue as well. Two women in the video is heard saying, "Oh, I would f--k [*student's name*]!" regarding two separate students. A male teacher can be heard saying, "I guess I'd bone [*student's name*]" as well. However, the school board's attorney was vehemently insistent that no teacher suggested anything sexual about any student.

Yeah, right.

Unfortunately, this was simply another example of school districts using whatever flimsy argument possible in order to minimize the issue of inappropriate teacher behavior. Many teachers feel that their behavior is protected by unions who shield their behavior and school boards who rationalize their misconduct, so as long as they lurk in the "gray areas," they have nothing to worry about.

When this video was made public, *no one* in the video was terminated. Three people resigned by choice and the rest remained employed with the school district, receiving only "verbal reprimands." And this punishment (or non-punishment) is nothing less than the school district subtly condoning this behavior. If there were ever "warning signs" of future inappropriate behavior, this sort of thing would be *Exhibit A*. And the most disturbing thing about the news reports regarding this was something the school officials told the media, saying, "There is no concern that the teachers will actually carry out what was said." *No concern*. And *that* is the mentality which perpetuates this epidemic.

But more often than not, there are warning signs.

---

150 The attorney's Kellyann Conway / Sean Spicer impression was dead-on.

Warning Signs

In a study commissioned by the Department of Education in 2004, Charol Shakeshaft explored, among many things, the warning signs of a teacher who may be having an inappropriate relationship with a student. She points out that the offending teachers are "often well liked and considered excellent teachers." This was true of me; along with the highly-rated evaluations of my teaching abilities from school and district administrators, I was also very popular among the students and staff. Also, teachers "who have access to students before or after school or in private situations" are more likely to commit these acts (such as coaches or music teachers). This coincides with another of Shakeshaft's points when she adds that a student might spend "increased time at school with one adult," and teachers may have "close personal relationships with students, time alone with students, time before or after school with students, time in private spaces with students, flirtatious behavior with students, and off-color remarks in class."

For the most part, I fulfilled all of those warning signs without even realizing it, and that was where the bulk of my fault resides. Thus, while Shakeshaft is absolutely correct about the warning signs of teachers who may be prone to sexual misconduct, my contention is that it is more often situational rather than motivational. While there *are* teachers who seek out student relationships, the majority of the sexual misconduct by teachers does not occur because they are predatory, but rather, because they become entrenched in their own cognitive distortions, creating an errant context in which certain behaviors are perceived as permissible. Teachers spend so much non-school(ish) time with students that they begin to view the students as peers rather than work products; teachers must have a guard of perspective, maintaining the proper mindset that students are students — perhaps best viewed as "clients" — maintaining boundaries which cover not only professional propriety, but social propriety as well.

The cognitive distortion I seemed to harbor during my relationship with my former student was the errant perspective that since I was only seeing her after school, she ceased to be a student because she neither sat in a desk nor did she appear on my attendance sheet. And naturally, I saw myself as one of those teachers who "isn't like that," or "I wouldn't do that," or "this wouldn't happen to me." That sort of thing was surreal and didn't actually happen, except in rumors and on TV, right?

There really is no way to predict which teachers will cross the lines of propriety; sometimes it's the teacher you most expect, and sometimes it's the teacher no one expects. However, the majority of teachers involved in sexual misconduct are referred to by Shakeshaft as "opportunistic abusers." These are *not* the fixated pedophilic predators one might envision when thinking about a teacher who has a relationship with a student. The "opportunistic abusers" are teachers "who aren't exclusively attracted to children or teenagers," and they "tend to be emotionally arrested and operate at a teenage level." That was me. Admittedly, I was a very immature adult while I was teaching and I enjoyed the social benefit of being viewed as a popular teacher. Shakeshaft continues:

> *The opportunistic abusers tend to spend a lot of time around groups of students, talking with them, going to the same places they go, and trying to blend in. They are the teachers who want to be seen as hip or cool and who want the students to think they are part of the student peer group. They are adults who comment on the attractiveness of the students, talking about a student as hot or sexy. Their conversations about students are often inappropriately personal. They also know a great deal about the personal lives of individual students, more than would be available to an adult whose interactions were academic or appropriately friendly (Shakeshaft, 2013).*

I didn't mind talking about the personal lives of students (though I don't remember ever randomly calling a student "hot" or "sexy"). I suppose I selfishly wanted to be *that teacher* who "changed the world" or something. I wanted to be John Keating. So I subtly made myself available to students — male and female — to talk about the intricacies of life, much of which included things I likely should have reported (such as drug abuse or underage drinking). But I didn't see it that way; I saw it as me being the teacher "they could talk to." But the reality was, with the things I was being told, it was my responsibility to send them to the school counselor, not be their sounding board.

It all comes down to mindset.

Situational vs. Opportunistic

While I understand the use of the word "opportunistic" in Shakeshaft's context, I think a more accurate word would be "situational." "Opportunistic" would imply the seizing of an opportunity, which isn't entirely accurate; "situational" more accurately describes the contextual and cognitive distortions experienced by the offending teacher when the line is crossed. Of course, this is strictly my opinion, from the inside of the situation, but it should carry some weight. I don't ever recall "seizing an opportunity," but rather, my recollection stems from a feeling of being "wrapped-up" in a situation which essentially got away from me — a situation I allowed to grow out of control by making the unreasonable seem reasonable, by making the insane seems sane, and by making the inappropriate seem appropriate.

I was certainly "situational," because in retrospect — having been away from the classroom for several years — I cannot fathom how any of my behavior could have ever seemed reasonable. And yet, at the time, for some reason,[151] it seemed completely reasonable; but it was completely insane.

---

151 i.e. – Cognitive Distortions.

CHAPTER NINETEEN

Sometimes, there is a whole other category to consider. Since this is a very complex and convoluted issue, multiple possibilities and perspectives exist; and all must be examined in order to gain a firm and full grasp on the situation. Limiting the scope of the issue will only limit the solutions of the problem, so all efforts must be made to see this complex subject from as many angles as possible.

Pathological

The issue of "opportunistic" or "situational" abusers does not apply when there is clear pathology involved. When the actions of a teacher go far beyond cognitive distortions and terrible choices, there is a much different variable to consider: Pathology — mental illness. Clearly, no teacher making reasonable and/or rational choices would partake in a relationship with a student. And when it does happen, the way to discern a situational instance from a pathological instance is the concept of *remorse*.

Beyond the initial interrogation following my arrest, I almost immediately admitted to what I'd done. There were some close friends with whom I took a bit longer to come clean, but for the most part, I was honest about my transgressions, never once justifying my actions or trying to make sense of my choices to anyone. Simply put, I was caught, I knew I was wrong, I knew what I'd done was wrong, and that was it; it was a situation that got away from me, and I had no one to blame but myself.

But when a teacher crosses over into pathology, they sing an entirely different tune. Pathological abusers will deny that their actions are "wrong" or will attempt to justify their actions, often seeking sympathy or even portraying themselves as the victim.

An Example

In probably one of the most notorious cases of pathology, Mary Beth Haglin, a substitute teacher from Cedar Rapids, Iowa went over-the-top with her scenario after her arrest.

Haglin was a long-term substitute high school English teacher; a tall, thin, attractive 24-year-old woman teaching at Washington High School in Cedar Rapids. She met the seventeen-year-old student at the school — in her role as teacher and his role as student — in the spring of 2015 when she substitute-taught at the high school. They met again the following fall and struck-up a friendship (which eventually morphed beyond propriety[152]). Over a brief span of time, the two began a sexual relationship ranging from the exchange of nude photos to sexual intercourse.

Following her July 2016 arrest, Haglin admitted the relationship took place, but did not admit fault. In fact, not only did she deny fault, she sought whatever public media outlet would listen in order to tell her side of the story. This eventually landed her on several nationally-televised programs.

In September of 2016, two months after her arrest, Haglin was profiled on *Inside Edition*, detailing the interactions between her and the student with whom she had the sexual relationship. She gave a detailed account of how they would meet regularly at a public park

---

152 Personally, I think a "friendship" between a student and a teacher is itself beyond propriety, but that is merely my opinion.

and have sex in either of their cars. Their sexual encounters, according to her, occurred on a nearly-daily basis.

"I never thought it would get this far," she said in her interview, "and I apologize so much." She said the student would leave her notes, including one referencing the movie *The Graduate*, which read, "Here's to you, Mrs. Robinson;" and others which said repeatedly, "I love you" and referred to her as his "empress." She then went on to say, "I realize now how stupid I was and what a terrible mistake I made," as she was interviewed for the show's segment.

However, a month later, in October, she was featured on *The Dr. Phil Show* telling an entirely different story. On this television appearance, her perspective completely changed.

"I was the victim," she said to Dr. Phil. Suddenly, everything was the student's fault. Departing from her apologetic tone on *Inside Edition*, Haglin began attributing her behavior to the student, not her own choices:

- "The student twisted my brain into accepting this relationship."
- "The student convinced me to send him sexy pictures; some nude."
- "The student is the one who seduced me."
- "He would always try and push all the limits, all of them."
- "He would grab me in his arms and he tried kissing me—"
- "It's not like I asked to enjoy it."

One thing she said to Dr. Phil which I do think is a common thread amongst teachers when it comes to the non-pathological cognitive distortions was when she remarked, "His age was erased in my mind." This statement, speaking from experience and extensive research, is a very common sentiment. Age *should* be a factor, but it is often the first casualty of the cognitive distortions because when the unreasonable becomes reasonable, facts become subjective.

Several things make the case of Mary Beth Haglin pathological rather than situational. First of all, her story changed rather dramatically. She literally went from remorseful to accusatory, first taking responsibility for her actions (referring to her choices as a "terrible mistake"), only to change her tone a month later and accuse the student of seducing her and convincing her and coming-on to her. Also, her relentless and shameless desire for publicity is quite suspect. Being featured on *The Dr. Phil Show* and *Inside Edition* seems (to me) a bit overboard considering she was merely being featured to tell her side of the story. There was no underlying message about the greater good or any sort of solution to what she'd done; in fact, the two accounts she gave on both programs were conflicting and nearly antithetical.

"...in my mind, this was a real relationship," Mary Beth Haglin said to Dr. Phil.

In the end, Mary Beth Haglin was convicted of *Sexual Exploitation by a School Employee* — a *misdemeanor* — and was sentenced to 90 days in jail.[153]

Justice.[154]

Another Example

A 55-year-old middle school P.E. teacher in my hometown was arrested for fondling a thirteen-year-old student in February of 2016. According to the Probable Cause Affidavit, Terry Couch took the student to his apartment where he took her to his bedroom. On the nightstand next to his bed, there was a framed picture of the girl — a selfie she'd posted on one of her social media pages. As they stood there, he proceeded to embrace her and hug her for five to eight

---

153 Not only did she receive a mere 90 days in jail for her ongoing sexual relationship with a high school student, but the judge told her that she did not have to immediately serve her sentence, advising her that it must simply be done within the following six months.

154 Insert eye-roll here…

minutes, caressing her body. And when he leaned in to kiss her, she pushed him away and said, "What the hell are you doing?"

After escaping his grasp, she ran outside to his car and climbed into his backseat, crying uncontrollably; Couch subsequently drove her home. Later that night, she sent him a text message, threatening suicide; to this he replied, "If you die, I die," followed by "I can't live without you." Couch had, in the past, referred to her as "Daughter" and "Beautiful" and once called her late at night to inquire about what she was wearing.

This man was nearly sixty-years-old; the girl was only thirteen.

This attraction is clearly pathological. This teacher did not become engulfed in a situation of cognitive distortions or self-delusion; he clearly became fixated on this young student regardless of her rejections of him and repeatedly attempted to cross the line. His words and deeds also were indicative that he was fully aware of her age and it seemed to be a motivating factor rather than something disregarded or overlooked. According to the affidavit, Couch told the girl in October of 2015, "If you were older, I would marry you;" a statement he made to her at least twice in-person and at least three times in text messages. Saying "If you were older…" clearly indicates his conscious awareness of her age. And yet, rather than being discourage by her age, it seemed to motivate him.

This is clear pathology.

In the end, Terry Couch's attorney and the prosecuting attorney agreed on a plea bargain in which Couch would plead no-contest to one count of *Aggravated Indecent Solicitation of a Child Under 14* — a *felony* — and the two attorneys agreed on a five-year term of probation. However, at Couch's sentencing hearing, the judge rejected this plea and sentenced Terry Couch to 32 months in state prison.

Justice.

A person who is attracted to someone underage specifically because of their age is mentally ill. However, this sort of perspective (or context) is not the typical case regarding teachers who embark on relationships with students. And that, in a nutshell, is the problem. When trying to remedy the issue, school officials, law enforcement, the public, and even other teachers want to approach the issue as though all offenders are pathological.

But the truth is, that is the exception, not the rule. And when the assumption is that all offending teachers are pathological or mentally ill, not only will teachers assume themselves to be immune from the situation, they will presume their colleagues — their *friends* — to be immune as well.

This is one of the paramount reasons why the problem persists.[155]

---

155   I cannot reiterate this point enough!

CHAPTER TWENTY

t's amazing what people can talk themselves into. It's amazing how some of the most outrageous and unthinkable actions can somehow, someway, seem like an option. It's amazing how, in one ever-so-brief moment, something absolutely ridiculous can all-of-a-sudden seem completely reasonable.

When my teaching career began, the notion of having a relationship with a student seemed as bizarre as it did ridiculous. I remember specifically being baffled by the mere logistics of such an absurd situation; *How could normal teacher-student interactions even mold into that sort of relationship?* It just seemed inconceivable. As a new teacher, from my perspective, I saw students come into my classroom, sit there during assignments, discussions, tests, etc., and then leave. *That was it.* I just couldn't envision a scenario when a teacher would say to a student, "It is not proper grammar to end a sentence in a preposition. Want to make out?" But I soon learned that it's not quite that cut-and-dry.

How it Happened

I met Taissa in 2008 when she was my student. She was in my International Baccalaureate English class, and she was, for the most part, an above-average student. We had a positive rapport, but nothing out-of-the-ordinary, and she produced solid B+ work in my class. She was one of those popular athletic smart girl types who seemed to cycle through friends and boyfriends with steady regularity. She socialized well and wasn't unusual in any particular respect. She had an athlete's physique and long blonde hair — she put me to mind of someone I would have been friends with in college.

There was simply nothing particularly eventful about our interactions while I was her teacher and she was my student. The year began, the year ended, and that was that. She was, in every way, just another student. But the following August, as a part of my Administrative Internship,[156] I was tasked with working at the fiasco of the annual end-of-summer enrollment for the upcoming school year.

For three days, I sat in the school gymnasium, assigned a task at a station, cycling students through the enrollment process. And as I sat at my assigned enrollment post, printing student ID cards, Taissa approached me and asked a favor which would change things forever.

"Brundage," She said, coming up behind me. Most students omitted the "Mr." from their salutation of me, and many had begun to call me *K.B.* Either way, I didn't mind.[157] "What's up?" she asked. "I need a favor."

I internally cringed. Usually, favors involved doing extra work.[158] "What can I do for you?" I asked with the faux-nicety I had mastered as a teacher.

"I have an open spot in my schedule. Can I be your proctor?"[159] She smiled.

---

156 Another part of my graduate school program for my M.Ed. in School Administration.

157 Or, more accurately, I merely didn't care; though it was nice to have a nickname.

158 Don't get me wrong, I wasn't a lazy teacher, but most of the time, doing more than I had to was quite off-putting. And yet, whenever someone asked for favor, I did it. I enjoyed being the guy that helped people out, be it faculty or student.

159 A proctor is what East High calls a Teacher Assistant (TA).

"Absolutely," I replied. I knew that she was intelligent and responsible (academically), and that is exactly the type of person I wanted as a Teacher Assistant because her tasks would include grading papers[160] and recording grades into the computer — tasks I'm pretty sure she really wasn't supposed to be doing — and any opportunity I had to offload some of the clerical nonsense of teaching was always a good idea.

"Great!" she said as I signed the form approving her request. "Thank you!" And she quickly walked away.

Over the next few months, Taissa worked diligently in my classroom, one hour a day, grading papers and entering grades into my computer, as well as any other random task I had. And, when needed, I gave her the hour to do homework she needed to get caught up on or a project she needed to finish. And often, we talked about life.[161]

Discussions

I didn't mind talking about the intricacies of life with my students. I think it was all part of my naïve compulsion to be John Keating. I wanted to be that teacher who someone said years later made a huge difference in their life.[162] Often, I had someone confide in me about something they were dealing with or struggles they were having,[163]

---

160 Mostly multiple-choice exams. I liked grading essays because I always assigned topics that interested me to make the grading a bit easier, but I also didn't mind having someone else grade the multiple-choice tests.

161 Mistake. Talking about life is why schools employ counselors. This was one of my first mistakes.

162 A few months after I was released from prison, one of my former students sent my wife a message on Facebook. When my wife asked if she was one of my students, she replied, "Yes I was. One that owes him a ton of thanks for helping get me through life stuff." When my wife showed me that message, it gave me an amazing feeling. I kind of did feel like John Keating.

163 When I was in court for my sentencing, I was criticized for this. It was brought up that I discussed sex with a female student. That's all the prosecutor said. The assistant district attorney said I was having inappropriate conversations with students because we were talking about sex. What he failed to mention to the judge was that the conversation about sex to which he was referring was a female student telling me that she was

and I felt a sense of worth — a sense that I was trusted. I felt like I mattered.[164]

Taissa was extremely open. Initially, the "How are you doing?" questions were answered casually and superficially, but eventually, she began to tell me nearly everything about her life. She told me about the drama she had with her friends; she told me about whatever new guy she was seeing; she told me about the parties she was going to and the drinking she was doing and the drugs she was trying — all I could do was give her the best feedback I could.[165] I told her that many of the things she was doing were things she would come to regret later, but she didn't seem to mind. It almost felt like she was telling me about her life because she needed a sounding board. So one day I asked her, "Why don't you talk to your parents the way you talk to me?"

"My parents would kill me," she replied. "They think I'm just their nice innocent daughter." She grinned a smirk full of context.

"Don't you get along with your parents?" I asked.

"Yeah," she replied, "when I see them."

"So they'd be upset if they knew the stuff you were doing?" I asked.

"Hell yeah," she replied quickly in a tone that implied it was obvious. "They're church people. They'd kill me if they knew I drank or smoked pot or wasn't a virgin."

Admittedly, this conversation should have made me uncomfortable, but it didn't. In retrospect, I think I had simply become so desensitized to the insanity of the adolescent drama rotating in and out of my

---

feeling pressured to have sex by her boyfriend; and I was telling her repeatedly not to go through with it. So yes, I talked to a female student about sex. I told her not to do it. But I guess the truth wasn't important to the prosecutor, only the way he could slant the details.

164 Notice how all these concepts were about me. Great Teacher vs. Teach Great

165 Actually, I should have referred her to the School Counselor.

classroom on a daily basis, nothing shocked me anymore.[166] So I did the smile-and-nod routine and gave her the most constructive feedback I could provide. I walked a fine line because I knew she was making some very destructive choices, but if I came down too hard with the "don't do that" message, I risked alienating my T.A. and not being seen as "cool," which was much more important to me and my ego.

About three months into the school year, Taissa informed me she would be transferring schools. She was in the International Baccalaureate (I.B.) program, but was tired of all the homework. She was only at Wichita East High School because of this academic program, and if she wasn't in I.B., she would be required to attend the school of the district in which she lived, which was on the south side of town. So on her last day, I bade her farewell and more-or-less never expected to see her again, although she was certain to tell me she'd keep in touch, which I doubted.

Apparently, my doubts were misplaced. That night, I was greeted by a Facebook "friend request" from her with a message that read, "I'm not your student anymore, so we can be Facebook friends!" And for reasons unknown to me then and now, I accepted the request.

Regular Visits

Over the next several months, she visited my classroom regularly after school, driving from her school to mine, just to see me. Ten minutes after my room was clear of students, Taissa would walk in, smiling and chatting. Honestly, I didn't mind her company. She typically helped me grade papers or straighten the room or organize textbooks. And this was when she became not only chatty, but excessively vocal about all aspects of her life. I'm not particularly certain how she saw me or what roll she felt I played in the narrative of her life, but whatever

---

166 Example from my Administrative Internship: A female student was called out of class by the police on a Monday morning because she was suspected of stabbing someone with a box knife over the weekend. When the police searched her, they found nothing. But then she went to the bathroom and tried to ditch the box knife in the tampon box in the ladies' room. A female administrator found the box knife. The student was hiding it in her vagina. Seriously. This type of thing was not unusual.

it was, it was enough that she told me nearly everything about every aspect of her existence.

Much of what she talked about for a long time was just the mundane driveling nonsense of a high school student, most of which I ignored as I worked away the afternoons in my classroom, wishing I was having one of my after-3PM encounters with one of my teacher hookups. But it was nice to have someone stop by who didn't mind doing the around-the-classroom tasks I'd been putting-off. At that point, I still had not even considered any sort of inappropriate relationship with her.

CHAPTER TWENTY-ONE

Spending so much time away from my wife took a major toll on our marriage. Many nights during my internship, I would arrive home when she was already in bed asleep, so I slept on the couch.[167] I felt emotionally and physically distant from her, and I'm really not sure why. None of this was her fault. I was the one being difficult; I was the one with the backwards priorities; I was the one having the affairs with other teachers.

At the time, the magnitude of my marital problems was not visible to me. Simply put, I was blinded; blinded by the women who made efforts to see me, engaged me in fun and stimulating conversations, and showed me what I believed to be genuine affection.

Nexus

This was the nexus of my worst cognitive distortions. I only saw Taissa socially and had no professional or educational interactions with her. I began to categorize her in my own flawed thought process as a peer, rather than a student or former-student.

---

167 I often refer to this as the only rough patch of our marriage, so neither of us quite knew how to handle it. I think it was another situation when she looked to me for guidance and I failed to be the leader of the relationship.

I could not see what was going on in my own life, because — in retrospect — I wasn't living my life; I was living a life that never happened in a reality that never existed. I managed to create a cognitively distorted world in my own mind which made the unreasonable seem reasonable, made the insane seem sane, and made the abnormal seem completely normal. However, this was not some sort of delusional mental illness, it was simply the extreme end of the contextual spectrum. Simply put, I viewed a student as a peer, and my boundaries with my peers were lacking.

That Night

One evening when I was the administrator-on-duty at a junior varsity basketball game,[168] Taissa called my cell phone[169] and asked if she could talk to me, in-person. She sounded distraught and I (of course) agreed and told her where I was, standing at the upper level of the gymnasium at East High School, nearly in the identical spot where she first asked me to sign the form allowing her to be my Teacher Assistant.

When she arrived, she was accompanied by her mother, so I knew something was wrong, and — with honest and good intentions — I offered to be someone with whom they both could speak and confide. On some levels, I felt happy and a bit empowered that they were seeking my advice on a situation.[170]

As they approached, her mother came up to me as Taissa stood back, pretending to watch the antics of junior varsity basketball.

---

168 As the intern, I typically worked the events the other administrators didn't want, which typically included weeknight junior varsity sports events.

169 She had my cell phone number. A lot of students did. This was a huge mistake on my part and definitely a blur in the line of teacher-student boundaries. But here's the thing: It's the norm. Teachers give out their cell numbers like it's no big deal. Teachers get texts from students all the time. Seriously, it's completely normal. Well, it's not normal, or at least it shouldn't be, but it's certainly the norm.

170 Again, it was about me.

"What's going on?" I asked her mom. I didn't immediately recognize her because we'd only met a few times at parent-teacher conferences, but my assumption that she was her mother was correct.

"Taissa wants to talk to someone, alone. And she mentioned you." She frowned. "Something happened with her boyfriend and she said she doesn't want to talk to me or her father about it, but she said she'd tell you."[171]

"Okay, we can talk. No problem," I replied with an eagerness to help.

When I approached Taissa, I tried to be friendly, but concerned. I didn't want to down-play anything, but our interactions were always so light-hearted, and being serious almost felt awkward.

"You okay?" I asked.

"I guess," she replied without looking up from the game. "I just need to talk. Can we go to your classroom?"

I looked around for the two security guards who were also supervising with me, and saw that they were both watching the crowd, so I walked her across the building to my room.[172]

We made the long walk to my classroom, barely saying a word, and when we went in, I shut the door and we both sat down on a small couch in the corner that I used for a silent reading area as well as someplace comfortable to grade papers after-hours, and even sometimes take a short nap.

---

171 This is something else I feel terribly about, because Taissa's mom literally brought her to me to confide in me because something was wrong and they hoped that I could help. But obviously, that didn't happen.

172 About my classroom: My room was on the far end of the third floor of the far west building of the colossal Wichita East High School campus. If anyone came to my classroom, it was because they had a reason. No one simply "passed by" my room. It was as isolated as a classroom could possibly have been in the building. This feeling of being apart from everything often made it difficult for me to interact with any staff members in other parts of the building – another thing that made me feel very alone as an individual.

Alone in the Classroom

When we sat down, she turned to me and seemed as though she needed me to prompt her before she could begin.

"What happened?" I asked.

She looked at me, tucking her long highlighted blonde hair behind her ears, and began her story.

"We were at Mikey's house, and we were making out in his room, and everything was normal." She paused, as though she wasn't sure how to continue, but she inhaled and kept going. "Like, randomly, during the stuff that we were doing, his mom knocked on the door. His mom doesn't speak English,[173] so he just said something to her through the door, and when she left, he got up and locked it."

Taissa paused, needing prompting again.

"Okay, then what happened?" I asked.

And she told me.[174]

Admittedly, this evoked several reactions in me.

First, I felt like someone had hurt a dear friend, and letting him get away with it seemed to me like the purest form of injustice. Throughout my teaching career, I developed a rapport with numerous students — male and female alike — of whom I had grown a little protective. She was one of them. On the other hand, my instincts told me this was not the whole story, and she wasn't being entirely honest, but I kept that sentiment to myself.

Second, it brought back harsh memories of my own similar instance, and fighting the bitterness of that memory as I tried to console her became an additional pressure I faced in the moment. In her moment of sadness, weakness, and vulnerability, I was harshly reminded of my own.

---

173 Mikey was Asian; Vietnamese if memory serves.

174 The details are not necessary, but they were details to which I could relate, considering what happened to me in the summer of 1998.

"And now," she continued, "I just don't know what I'm going to do. I wish I had said something, but I didn't, and now I just feel like I can't talk to anyone."

As I listened to her, she leaned her head on my shoulder and I put my arm around her, trying to offer an awkward sense of comfort. When she stopped talking, I wasn't sure what to say, so I let silence blanket the room. I was torn between feeling emotionally empowered as she was willing to tell me something deeply personal, and feeling emotionally vulnerable as I was hearing a story that seemed to partially mirror my own.

As the silence became deafening and she held her head on my shoulder, she didn't move. She didn't move until she slowly looked up at me and we made direct and very close eye contact.

Broken Silence

There was a crashing sea of emotion in the room, and it was only building more with every second as she looked to me for support. She stared into my eyes, and I stared back. And then, as though we were in some sort of movie with the quintessential intensifying music reaching a crescendo in our minds, our faces began to slowly draw closer together.

"Is this really happening?" I whispered.

"Yes," she replied, nodding gently.

And then, her cell phone rang.

I'm not really a hands-to-the-heavens Christian, but sometimes I wonder if God talks to us. We, of course, don't get the booming voice Moses and Noah got, but maybe God gives us (for lack of better words) signs and hints at defining moments of our lives.

That cell phone call was one of those moments.

"It's my mom," she said before answering, looking uncomfortably at the caller-ID display.

I took a very deep breath and tried to bring myself back into reality, grasping for an understanding of what was happening; trying to clutch any logical reasoning behind the events unfolding, but found nothing.

"Okay, Mom. Just a few more minutes," she said, and she hung up.

That moment — *that call* — was probably the defining moment of my entire existence. Had I decided to stand up at that moment and walk her back to the gym, perhaps none of this would have happened. At that moment, I thought I was in control of what would become the defining moment of my entire life.

I was being tested, and I failed.

She placed her cell phone on the floor next to the couch, and we seemingly and seamlessly reassumed the exact position we were in prior to the phone call.

Once again, silence blanketed the room as we looked at each other once more.

And then, we kissed.

Flawed Reality

I like to think I have a pretty solid grasp on the world; I like to think I know what's going on around me; I like to think the events in my general vicinity make sense and my decisions and reactions to these events do — more often than not — concurrently make sense.

During the four weeks our relationship lasted, reality contemporaneously made perfect sense and no sense. My marriage felt like it was crumbling, but I somehow didn't mind. I was having an emotional and somewhat physical affair with a 15-year-old girl, immediately after casually ending an affair with another teacher, and having several other casual affairs with other teachers; and this seemed perfectly normal and acceptable to me. I was sleeping on the couch at night, away from my wife, and I was making out in classrooms and cars with my (at-the-time) teacher flings.

This should have bothered me, but it didn't. I just rolled with it. Everything that I thought was real was false, and the only firm reality I had in my life was slowly slipping away. This was the deepest depths of my cognitive distortions. I was in *The Matrix*. Nothing was real, but in its own way, everything was real.

During our four-week fling, Taissa and I actually went on a few "sort-of" dates. We went and worked-out together at the YMCA, we went for a long walk in a park; we even went out to eat together, in public. And this just all seemed fine to me because it was part of the distortion. It didn't seem real, but it didn't seem out-of-the-ordinary either. It just, simply, *was*. But eventually, things began to change.

My perspective began to clear up about half-way through the third week of my fling with Taissa. She began to drop little one-liners at me that I'm sure she thought were completely innocuous, but to me, felt like an anvil on my chest.

"So how's my secret boyfriend?" she sometimes asked when she would call.

"I like our secret relationship," she said to me once, out-of-the-blue.

"You're my favorite felon," she said after one of our four physical exchanges.

This was the type of thing that began to put it into perspective. These phrases spawned a cognitive process that brought my entire reality into question. I had a solid moment of clarity, and I realized I had been spending the last four weeks living impulse to impulse, without respect for any of the consequences.

Early one Saturday morning, we met for breakfast after she finished with some church function she was doing, and afterwards, we sat in my car and made-out for a while. But this time it was different. The three previous times, there was a happier motif, but this time, the feel of the whole scenario was more intense and, for some reason, kind of dark. Neither of us smiled much and when we were done, we parted ways with that awkward, "Well, see you later."

That was the night I confessed everything to my wife.

Ended

I fought myself for over a week on how to end it. And it wasn't before long that things started happening that confirmed my decision to end things. First, Taissa's incessant uses of "secret boyfriend" and "secret relationship" allusions were forcefully driving me toward my decision. But at the same time, she was also switching back-and-forth between placing me in the "secret boyfriend" roll or the "trusted mentor" roll because she began confiding in me the complications that were arising with the other two guys with whom she was having a physical relationship. This never made me jealous, obviously, but it did bring the situation into a much greater perspective and brought my reality back down to Earth. I needed to get out.

When it ended, it was unremarkable. It was a conversation, an agreement, and a conclusion. That was it. We both agreed that the relationship was a mistake and we wanted to remain friends, and for a while, we did.

But then I got a job teaching at another school, in another district, several hours away. I moved out of town, doing everything I could to leave the past behind. But Taissa didn't like that idea, so one morning in August of 2011, I awoke to an email from her:

"I hate you. I hate you for acting like you moving away helps you move away from everything you've ever done. Well guess what. I'm stuck here, when I should be the one moving to run away from everything. I was fine with myself for a while. And then when i saw that you were leaving, and HAPPY, none the less, to get away from baggage, i was filled with anger. And i can't even tell you how bad i've wanted to say something. I held it back for so long, and i just can't do it anymore. You think it's okay to just run? Like, your world is filled with rainbows and sunshine? Yeah. Mine's not. I still think about what happened sometimes when i'm driving by myself or i pass east. Nothing will ever erase those awful memories. No matter where i go.

No matter who i'm with. And i hate you for acting like you moving allows you to escape. I hope you have a wonderful time in lawrence. I hope you love that school. But i'll never be able to forgive myself. And i feel like no matter what i do to attempt to forget, it always comes back. And there's no one i can talk to about it, so now i have to sit here and just think to myself. In circles. Over & over & over. Which only makes it worse. So thank you, so much."

The message scared me — for months. Every time I saw a police car drive by our house in Lawrence, I wondered if that was the day everything would come crashing down. I lived in an internal prison of my own fear and paranoia. Every time I felt like I was feeling better about life, I reminded myself of how my past could easily (and without warning) show up and take away everything I loved. And even though I was happy and content with my new life at my new school, I knew there was always a chance my old life would come back to haunt me.

And it did.

I was arrested seven months later.

CHAPTER TWENTY-TWO

Right now, at this exact point in the Space-Time Continuum, I'm sitting in a Subway Sandwich Shop, typing on my laptop computer. It's cold in here, probably because it's hot outside, and this Subway smells like every other Subway on the planet. The line of people stretches from the glass-covered food line to the entrance of the store, each patron eagerly awaiting his/her sandwich, prepared with each specific individual detail they would like on their otherwise-ordinary sandwich.

I suppose that's something I like about Subway. Each sandwich starts as a base sandwich — a tuna sandwich, for example — but from there, anything is possible. There are literally thousands of different tuna sandwiches at Subway, just as there are thousands of versions of each available sandwich, because Subway is the quintessential culinary metaphor for individuality. As I hear each patron in the soundscape, asking for each of their individual ingredients, details, preferences — white or wheat bread or flat bread; tuna or spicy Italian or club or meatball marinara — this place is the perfect display of individuality, wrapped in paper and served with a beverage.

A Subway sandwich is the perfect metaphor of how one thing can be experienced from so many varying aspects, none of which is superior to the other, all of which are relevant.

Subway is my current locale because it is where a man has agreed to be interviewed for this book. Again, at this current juncture in the Space-Time Continuum, *After 3PM* is essentially done, except for *this* chapter. But Subway is also the perfect microcosm of this chapter's purpose. All throughout my experiences and research regarding this issue, I have explored the manner in which teachers are impacted by teacher-student relationships, I've explored the way it damages teachers' families and careers, and I've also explored the manner in which students are impacted as well. But there is a fourth dimension to this aspect: The students' families.

Seeing each new instance of unlawful teacher-student relationships on television prompts anger toward the teacher, sympathy toward the student, but the people caught in the middle of this — the student's family — can often be overlooked.

I happen to know one such family.

The manner in which I am acquainted with the man I'm about to interview is not important. I offered him the courtesy of complete anonymity in his discussion with me, so there will be no specific details about his individual ordeal. I will only provide these general facts: A few years ago, his son had a sexual relationship with his female teacher. This relationship came to light, the teacher was fired and arrested, and the boy and his family were left to pick up the pieces. Beyond that, the specifics are not important. Because right now, as I sit in Subway, waiting for him to arrive, I have no interest in what his son did or the fate of his teacher. The information I seek is deeper than that; he is going to tell me how the unlawful teacher-student relationship in which his son was a part nearly blew-up his entire family.

I do not yet have an alias for him, because I will obviously not be using his name. So I think I will give him the name of whatever actor or film/television character he reminds me.

The Fourth Dimension

As Frank[175] approaches my table from over my left shoulder, I promptly stand, we greet with a smile and a handshake, and I am again reminded (as I am nearly every time we meet) of how short he is; no taller than 5'8" if my estimate is correct. In retrospect, I always remember him as taller because of the amount of respect I have for him. I know what this man has been through, and he has still managed to persevere with a successful life and a charitable heart.

When I first arrived at Subway, I sought a table which would provide us with some privacy, but with the placement of these tables, this becomes difficult. I offer to switch tables and he agrees, so after buying him his own individual sandwich as well as my own, we situate ourselves at a secluded(ish) table, seated diagonal from one another, and I come to a difficult realization: I don't recall ever having interviewed anyone like this. So, doing my best to recall as much of *All the President's Men* as I could, I attempted to emulate the demeanor and tone of Woodward and Bernstein.

Frank seems uncomfortably relaxed as he eats his toasted ham sub. I'm pretty sure it's my job to put the interviewee at ease so that he feels comfortable talking to me (even though I've been friends with Frank for several years), so with no other starting point in my mind, I decided to ask about "the beginning."

A bit more detailed background: When Frank's son was in high school, he had sex with his high school teacher, an attractive twenty-

---

175 I have decided to give my interviewee the name "Frank." He reminds me of Brecken Meyer, one of the actors in Franklin & Bash, one of my favorite sit-coms. In this show, Brecken Meyer plays the character of Jared Franklin. However, giving my interviewee the alias of Jared would be weird, since we're sitting in Subway and Subway Jared ended up being a pretty creepy fellow. So instead of Franklin, I'll shorten that to Frank. Therefore, Frank it shall be. Besides, on Franklin & Bash, Franklin was much more awesome than Bash.

something woman who taught English. The teacher was subsequently arrested, fired, charged with Unlawful Sexual Relations, and pled-down to a charge which earned her probation and did *not* require registration as a sex offender.[176]

"How did you find out?" I asked, realizing my timing for this question wasn't ideal since he'd just taken a sizeable bite of his sandwich.

"Well," he said, raising his eyebrows as though the memory had reintroduced itself into his psyche and he was a little surprised to be reacquainted, "I got a phone call at work from my son, and he said, 'Dad, you're going to get a call to come to the school for a meeting with the principal,' and he said there was an issue with a teacher." Frank stared out the window for a moment and the skin between his eyes crinkled in contemplation. "And honestly," Frank continued, "I didn't know what exactly it was about. He said there was an issue with a teacher that had become public and we needed to come to the school for a meeting."

When Frank and his wife attended this meeting, he said he was under the impression that it would be informal because it was an off-the-record discussion with some school officials. So, on his way to the meeting, Frank and his wife were concerned, but also puzzled.

The meeting occurred after school, so the school building was, for the most part, deserted and some of the hallways were dark. In the distance, the occasional clang of a slamming locker could be heard, but not seen. Upon entering the room where this meeting would be held, Frank introduced himself to the principal, a member of the school board, and a police officer, all of whom seemed to look at him and his wife with expressions of sympathy. Frank could feel the uncertainty in his mind morph quickly into a sense of unknowing, unsure, and uncomfortable.

"Well," the police officer began, "we have been investigating an instance of a possible molesting encounter with a teacher."

---

176 See Chapter Seventeen.

This was the moment when everything changed. This was the moment when it became real. This was the moment when Frank realized why each person was looking at him as they were — not with looks of sympathy, but with looks of concern, as the parents of a victim.

For the next several hours, Frank and his wife sat and discussed the details of the sexual encounter their son had with his English teacher. With each passing minute, the air seemed still, but heavy. Tension and nervousness was quickly replaced by embarrassment and shame.

Laying the Blame

"I felt like I'd failed somehow as a parent,"[177] Frank tells me as we both peer over our Subway sandwiches at whatever is behind the other; I can tell he's serious, but I can also tell that it still bothers him, years later. His eyes are staring blankly into the past as he recalls that meeting, remembering not only the sights he saw, but the feelings he felt. It's almost as if he could still feel that room, and if he were to ever reenter that room, he would feel that same uneasiness all over again.

No one ever forgets the place where everything changed.

"But I also feel like it was both of their faults," he interjects, speaking of his son and the teacher. "I think they were equally at fault, but I hold the teacher more accountable and I hold the school system accountable for having teachers who aren't prepared; something needs to be done to lessen this."

I sat back in my chair and took a breath, seeing as how this was one of the last things I expected to hear — Frank essentially told me *my own* philosophy — the philosophy of *After 3PM* — which was *his* reaction to his own son having a relationship with a teacher.

"I just think," Frank continued, pausing for a moment, "she should have gotten more punishment. If the gender roles were reversed, this would have been a completely different story and the teacher would

---

177 Coincidentally, both my parents told me this exact same thing.

have been dealt-with completely different."[178] He shook his head in disappointed disbelief, and we moved on with the discussion.

Frank said his initial reaction to the ordeal, as the parent of a student who had an affair with a teacher, was that of shame and embarrassment within the community. However, he tells me that this was quick to change.

"Well," he said with a sigh, "we held a lot of shame, but it really turned to anger with my son." He paused; I could see some of this residual anger cross his countenance. "I mean, I know he was in high school, but he still should have known better." He paused again, shaking his head slightly and returning his distant stare to the oblivion of the past. "And like I said," he continued, "it made us feel like we failed somewhere as parents."

At this moment, I wanted to provide some sort of consoling or comforting words, but I wasn't sure how that would sound coming from . . . *me*. So I let Frank continue.

Subway was steadily emptying-out as the lunch rush began to slow; the restaurant grew a bit quieter.

"Yeah, he was definitely old enough to know better," Frank tells me with stern resolve in his voice, nodding his head slightly. He leaned back in his chair, as if to emphasize how certain he was about the point he was about to make. "My son was smart enough to know not to do something stupid like that," he said, still nodding his head, "so I do blame the teacher, but I also blame my son."

This caught me somewhat off-guard, so I needed a visual aid here. Maybe I was having trouble grasping the fact that the parent would be upset with his son — the student — but as Frank kept talking, it made more and more sense.

"Well," I said, attempting to create this visual aid in my mind, "on a pie chart, what percentage do you, as the parent, place on your son and what percentage do you place on the teacher?"

"50/50," Frank replied with immediacy and without hesitation.

---

178 Like I said, see Chapter Seventeen.

I stopped for a moment, somewhat speechless, but definitely silent. In this moment of silence, I tried to stare at my laptop computer screen like I was formulating the next question, but I was actually asking myself if Taissa's parents could have been mad at her for what she and I had done together, and if so, I suddenly felt even worse about the situation because, at that moment, I knew this may have been just one more way I'd hurt her — my immediate fear was that I'd damaged her relationship with her family.

And then I thought of my own daughter and how she will be in high school soon. And then I couldn't think about it anymore. I just couldn't.

"Well," I said to Frank, "I didn't expect that answer." We both smiled uncomfortably.

Fallout

The following few months were filled with tension and uncertainty for their family. Both Frank and his wife had difficulties at their jobs; lack of sleep, lack of concentration, and even the knowledge that their coworkers knew exactly what their family was going through, yet nearly no one spoke to them about it or tried to console them. Their coworkers only spoke about it amongst themselves.

This also became an issue at their church. The church family they'd grown to love — most (or all) of whom were also aware of what was going on with Frank's son and the teacher as the legal battles and media coverage seemed to increase by-the-day — appeared to turn a blind conscience to the issue. No one offered prayers, no one offered hugs, no one offered comforting words of consolation; the church seemed to pretend like the biggest (and most public) struggle Frank's family had ever encountered was simply not happening. It was as though the church existed within its own confined reality, and nothing from the outside world could penetrate the humdrum of Sunday mornings. Of course, the members of the church had plenty to say about the events involving Frank's son and the teacher, but it was all said in whispers and behind the backs of those involved. Needless to say, Frank and his family left the church soon after.

At home, tensions began to rise in the weeks and months following the teacher's arrest. Seeing her picture on the news with alarming regularity, Frank struggled with the notion that his son was one of the victims of this teacher's tragic and destructive choices; but Frank's struggles went deeper. Frank struggled with anger; of course, he was angry with the teacher whom he trusted as an educator, but he was also angry with his son.

"So," I said, "as a family, how did it impact you guys; how did it impact your family dynamic?"

"Well," he said, looking up in contemplation, "it put a huge cloud over graduation." He reminded me that this occurred in the March/April timeframe, just as his son was about to graduate. Essentially, Frank told me, his son's graduation from high school has become unfortunately synonymous with these events, making it an unenjoyable experience and a forgettable memory.

I looked down at my computer screen again, pretending to read something that wasn't there. *How many of Taissa's life events did I ruin? How many arguments and humiliating circumstances did I create for Taissa's family? How badly did I scar her otherwise-happy memories?* I kept a straight face as Frank kept talking, but I was feeling lower and lower by the second.

"Counseling helped," Frank said, pulling me from my cognitive quicksand.

"You went to counseling?" I asked, switching back to writer-mode.

"Yeah, for several months," he nodded. "At first it was the three of us,[179] then it was just my son." I could tell from the look on Frank's face that he wasn't sure whether or not the counseling had helped his son, but he'd always hoped it did.

---

179 Frank, his wife, and their son. I can only imagine how difficult those sessions were, and I wondered if Taissa ever had to do anything similar.

"Then he left for college," Frank continued, "but that didn't work out. He dropped out after only a year, and now he's living at home, trying to figure out what he wants to do with is life."

Moving On

"We managed to move out of town," Frank tells me with a sense of resolve. "I wouldn't say that this incident was the reason we moved, but it was certainly a contributing factor." He seemed content with that and didn't regret his decision, though I can see in his eyes that the trudging of these memories was wearing him down. I can tell that it's growing increasingly difficult to talk about his son, and that Frank really does still carry some guilt and blame about the situation. However, being one of the most personable men I've ever met, he does his best to not let it show.

My next question would have been to ask if the relationship his son had with his teacher somehow altered his son's worldview in such a negative way that he was struggling to grasp the values and priorities of adulthood. But instead, I decided to start bringing the interview to a conclusion. On many levels, I consider this man a friend, and was not about to wear-out my welcome.

"So, is it a topic of conversation anymore?" I ask.

"No, not really," he replied. His voice was tired.

"How long was there an elephant in the room for your family? I mean, how long did this unspoken topic feel like it lingered?"

"About two-and-a-half years," he said. "We've dealt with it, but the issue is still there."

Hearing him say that he'd dealt with it was comforting to me; the entire conversation between Frank and me made me think of Taissa's family. I couldn't help but parallel the pain and struggles Frank's family experienced, knowing I'd caused that same pain to another family as well.

On the other hand, Frank has been able to forgive everyone, which I think is a huge testament to his character, and that too gave me hope. He lives every day knowing someone caused him and his family a considerable amount of pain, whereas I live every day knowing I caused that pain to another family.

And with that knowledge alone, it blows my mind that Frank is willing to be my friend.

Otherwise-Extraordinary

Some people have enough ingredients in their character which transform an otherwise-ordinary person into the extraordinary person they become. I suppose my conversation with Frank has really made me understand the sandwich metaphor. We are all otherwise-ordinary people living otherwise-ordinary lives; what makes us unique is what we add to our lives, how we flavor our lives, and what we include (or do not include) in our lives. Frank chose not to add bitterness and resentment, and instead, he chose to add forgiveness — and that tends to make for a much tastier sandwich.

I wanted to have this conversation with Frank to learn about the family's perspective when they are forced to deal with an unlawful teacher-student relationship. But Frank has shown me something beyond that. Frank has proven that people like me can be forgiven by those who are the most justified in maintaining anger and resentment.

I know Taissa's parents are Christians, and I sometimes wonder if they forgive me for what I've done. I may disagree with Frank's 50/50 assignment of blame, but that's his opinion as a father; I assign myself much more blame than that.

But most of all, Frank has shown me that throughout the sex scandal they had to endure, their family survived; and I guess I just really hope Taissa's family survived too.

CHAPTER TWENTY-THREE

For all intents and purposes, I really should have been caught sooner. In retrospect, during the four-week span of my relationship with Taissa, I have no idea how the other teachers in my hallway could have overlooked the fact that she was coming to my classroom nearly every day after school. To be clear (once again): what I did was *not their fault*, but this "Not my business/Not my problem" nonsensical mindset must stop.

Speak Up

One thing Charol Shakeshaft mentions in her report is that rumors or suspicions should be reported, no matter what:

> *Policies should stress that any report, rumor, or suspicion of sexual misconduct must be reported to the responsible authorities. Policies should stress that reporting suspected misconduct is both a professional responsibility and the law. Individuals who report suspected abuse are not responsible for determining the validity of the suspicion — that's the role of the subsequent investigation by police or child service workers (Shakeshaft, 2013).*

However, the problem with this is how it is handled once the report is made (which is a whole other issue entirely). But teachers must be vigilant about the safety and well-being of students, even if it means forsaking their professional loyalties to a colleague. And honestly, if the colleague is genuinely doing nothing wrong, he/she has nothing to worry about; and if the colleague is on his/her way to making some destructive decisions, a stern reality-check could easily be motivation enough to reexamine a few things (such as mindset and context).

One of the biggest problems, however, is teachers' insistence on not rocking the boat. There is an inherent fear of "getting involved" with a problem which is leading to this *head-in-the-sand* mentality.

Here is an example: During my first year of teaching, I was standing in the hallway with some older teachers (one of whom was actually my teacher when I went to school there) and they were talking and gossiping as usual. And the topic of a former colleague who was then at another school came up. And one teacher, my former teacher, said, "One day I walked in his classroom, and he had a girl pinned against the wall and they were doing god-knows-what; so I just turned around and left. Not my business."

This is negligence at its worst. I knew the teacher he was talking about, and these allegations did not surprise me in the least. But what *did* surprise me was his insistence that it wasn't his "business" to get involved and not report it. This perspective genuinely blew my mind and I could not believe what I was hearing as I listened to this conversation. However, judging from the reaction of the other teachers in the discussion, it was their opinion that "not getting involved" was the right decision.

I can't help but think that *this* was one of the paramount reasons I was not caught at the time. I simply cannot fathom how my colleagues could not have noticed this former student visiting me after school every day, and not saying anything (or at least wondering anything). They should have reported to the principal that a male teacher was having a female student in his classroom after school regularly.[180] The principal should have had a one-on-one meeting with the teacher to kindly and professionally remind him that there is a slight appearance of impropriety and, while no accusations are made, it is best to keep all appearances above reproach. And more-often-than-not, this small reality check can make all the difference. Context is everything, and sometimes a subtle reminder of contextual reality can shatter the cognitive distortions.

It *should* be common sense, but it's *not*. Something more must be done.

Stop-Look-Listen-Act

So, here's the thing: Stop — Look — Listen — Act. I understand that teachers are often overloaded, hectically moving from one task or responsibility to another, and many of the subtle clues and details of impropriety are easily missed. When occupational tunnel-vision sets in, we often don't notice anything beyond the next pressing thing on our to-do lists. Therefore, the key is simply taking a moment and evaluating the setting of your story, examining the supporting actors of your film, and paying attention to the subplots you may have missed.

A teacher-student relationship has happened (or is happening) in nearly every high school (and many middle schools) in America. That is a simple and unfortunate fact. So knowing how to thwart these instances is vital to maintaining a safe and secure learning (and working) environment.

1. Stop — If teachers would take a moment and observe the behaviors of their colleagues as much as they observe their students, much of this behavior could be addressed before students are harmed. It isn't the mentality of "catching"

---

180 As I must make this declaration once again, I do not blame anyone for the choices I made. It is not the fault of my colleagues for what I did. Sorry, but this repeated disclaimer is needed.

another teacher doing something inappropriate, but rather, keeping one another accountable. There's a reason it's called the "educational *community*." Faculties are families who go through so much together; turning a blind eye to things that are "not my business" or not wanting to "get involved" by simply ignoring impropriety can only be described as irresponsible and dangerous.

2. Look — If teachers see something that seems improper, something needs to be said immediately. This, of course, is a slippery slope depending on numerous variables such as the teacher's relationship with his/her colleagues, the reporting teacher's relationship with the administrators, or even the administrators' relationship with the teacher being reported. Thus, each instance must be evaluated and handled individually. However, the only option that is *not* an option is inaction. Seeing a potential problem and doing nothing only perpetuates the problem. In this instance, inaction is tantamount to negligence.

3. Listen — More often than not, rumors carry at least some semblance of truth. In most cases, rumors don't start from nothing; and while many rumors are exaggerations or assumptions, it does not mean they are not rooted in some percentage of truth. For example, a teacher may not be crossing any lines of propriety with a student, but if someone at some point got the impression that this was happening based solely on observation, then perhaps the teacher needs to reevaluate his/her interactions with students to prevent this perception from causing problems, or prevent him/herself from entering any compromising situations or developing cognitive distortions.

4. Act — Teachers, it *is* your business; it *is* your responsibility. Plainly-said, if a teacher is not breaking the rules or crossing the line, he/she has nothing to worry about if colleagues raise

concerns. Sometimes the mere appearance of impropriety is enough to cause problems, so raising those concerns with school administrators is a necessity. If an administrator needs to have a sit-down discussion with a teacher about appearances and perceptions, then so-be-it. Better to risk possibly offending someone than to ignore the warning signs until another relationship hits the news.

Protocol

Unfortunately, many schools do not have a specific protocol in place to handle these situations, specifically when reports are based on rumors, suppositions, or suspicions. As a result, much of this behavior goes undetected or unreported. Therefore, there must be a system in place to deal with these situations. As Charol Shakeshaft stated in her report:

> *Selecting one person to whom all school personnel must report any rumor, allegation, complaint, or suspicion is helpful in insuring that no student falls through the crack and patterns of misconduct are quickly and effectively identified. However, because the designated employee may engage in misconduct, a school district or school may want to assign more than one employee to handle allegations of educator sexual misconduct and have these employees coordinate their efforts to identify any patterns of behavior (Shakeshaft, 2004).*

These designated individuals could be assistant principals, respected teachers, school counselors, or even trusted outside individuals. But regardless of who is given this role and/or responsibility, it is vital for schools to have a protocol and an individual (or individuals) to deal with rumors, subtle allegations, or reasonable suspicions. Honestly, as a teacher, had I been inclined to report a teacher for sexual misconduct, I do not know who I should have spoken to, the actions

I should have taken, or the process to follow. As a teacher, I was never informed on any policy or protocol regarding the reporting of other teachers. Sure, we were given plenty of training regarding the latest educational strategy based on whatever book was read by some face-less district advisor. However, regarding student safety, any training was limited to the scope of abuse or neglect from parents, the use of drugs or alcohol, or involvement in gangs and/or violent behavior; reporting teacher misconduct was never addressed.

It all comes down to accountability. It has nothing to do with trust or distrust, like or dislike, competence or incompetence — it's about student safety and staff accountability. School and district safeguards must exist (or be enforced, if they already exist) which require teachers to report even the suspicion of impropriety.

"Policies should stress that any report, rumor, or suspicion of sexual misconduct must be reported to the responsible authorities," Shakeshaft wrote in 2013. "Policies should stress that reporting suspected misconduct is both a professional responsibility and the law."

The educational community can no longer afford to assume this problem is an "other-world" problem. These acts of abuse are occurring every day at every level — public schools, private schools, parochial schools — so the assumption that it only happens at schools such as [insert assumption here] is simply naïve and incorrect. It is an everywhere problem.

There is a certain amount of arrogance which prevents schools, teachers, and principals from addressing this issue within their own walls. The assumption that "it simply doesn't happen at our school" is dangerous and borderline-negligent. A brief examination of the varying schools in which teacher sexual misconduct has occurred proves the unfortunate diversity of schools impacted by this epidemic. So the presumption that it does not impact certain schools in certain settings with a certain racial-makeup or socioeconomic status is errant and dangerous.

And yet, the most dangerous aspect of this issue in the public eye is not the number of teachers on the news or the front page of newspapers, it is the number of teachers not caught, never accused, and never ever held accountable. More teachers are getting away with sexual misconduct than are getting caught. And although law enforcement and school administrators can (and do) play a role in attacking this problem head-on, it is imperative for teachers and school staff to be as vigilant about keeping their colleagues accountable as they are keeping students accountable. Teachers are not above suspicion, and there should be no "loyalty" when it comes to student safety, especially regarding teacher sexual misconduct. Turning the blind-eye and not reporting a colleague out of some sort of occupational loyalty should be criminally prosecutable. In prison, people don't "snitch" because of the likely repercussions. Why do teachers — in schools, teaching students — adopt this same mentality?

Say Something

Honestly, I wish someone had reported me when my behavior was merely suspicious. There were warning signs in my own behavior long before I ever crossed the lines of legality. And here's the thing: The things I was doing — the simple warning signs — broke no rules, violated no laws, nothing. However, if someone had reported my behavior to our principal, and the principal had a stern sit-down discussion with me about the perceptions being drawn from my behavior, I have no doubt that I would have refocused my perspective, stepping back and reevaluating the situations feeding my own cognitive distortions. Perhaps, I would not have made the choices I made.[181] Sometimes, protecting one another from ourselves is the best way to protect students. But that takes the vigilance and willingness to step beyond workplace friendships and loyalties to place student

---

181 Once again, it is not the fault of anyone except me for making the choices I made regarding the relationship I had with my former student. And I must again reiterate this point – again.

safety above all else. And if the teacher in-question is above reproach, he/she has nothing to worry about. If the teacher is violating the law, he/she should be investigated and turned-over to law enforcement. If the teacher has not yet crossed any lines, he/she will (at the very least) be given the opportunity to correct behavior raising questions and maintain better professional conduct.

Any teacher approached by another staff member regarding this issue (or any questionable behavior) should *never* be offended. These conversations must take place from the perspective of helping the teacher establish the appropriate perceptions through appropriate behavior in appropriate contexts. And teachers who feel the need to report their colleagues must shed this fear of offending their fellow teacher; student safety must be the top priority. This informal fraternity of teachers who look-out for one another regardless of their behavior is a trend which is every bit as dangerous as the teachers who are crossing the lines of legality.

Failing to report teacher misconduct is every-bit as dangerous as the conduct of the offending teacher.

What to Watch

The warning signs are obvious. And although it works both ways, consider it in the context of a male teacher:[182]

- Does the teacher seem to get more-than-normal attention from the female students?
- Does the teacher routinely give out his cell phone number and receive text messages from these students?
- Does the teacher seem to spend more of his spare time at school with these students in a social context rather than in an academic context or with other teachers?
- Does the teacher see these students in his classroom after school?

---

182 This remains accurate if gender roles are reversed.

- Does the teacher interact with these students outside of school?
- Have there been rumors about the teacher and other members of the faculty being sexually involved?
- Does the teacher appear to care more about being a "cool" teacher instead of being an effective teacher?
- Does the teacher take pride in his popularity among the student population?
- Is the teacher having problems in his personal life?
- Does the teacher reveal details about his personal life to his students?
- Is the teacher particularly lenient with the students regarding his enforcement of school policy?

More often than not, suspicions are correct; these suspicions need to be reported to the school administration *every time*. These conversations with administrators should occur with the full understanding that the administrator *will not* reveal his/her source about these suspicions. And each suspicion should be approached as a matter of concern, *not* an allegation.

But still, I can't help but wonder, if my principal had come to me and said, "There seems to be an appearance of impropriety," prior to me crossing the line with Taissa, perhaps I would have had the opportunity to step back, analyze my behavior, and realize how deep my cognitive distortions had gotten; perhaps it would have been the jolt I needed to regain my priorities.[183]

I've given up trying to figure out the *what-could-have-been* for my own life, but I am determined to impact the *what-could-be* in the lives of others.

---

183 Of course, it is not the administration's fault for not saying anything to me. As I've said repeatedly, I was responsible for the choices I made. However, this plan of action could be the difference-maker for a teacher in the future who may be toeing the same dangerous line.

CHAPTER TWENTY-FOUR

On spring afternoons, I can still hear Shakespeare in my ears. Every year I taught at Wichita East High School, my alma mater, William Shakespeare's *Romeo & Juliet* was always the final thing I would teach at the end of the year. We would read (and perform) the play in class, or listen to the audio and follow-along with the play in the big thick orange textbook. And with every Act completed, the class would view the Leonardo DiCaprio version and we'd have great discussions about parallels and symbolism and plot devices and Shakespearian history — and life.

> Why then, O brawling love! O loving hate!
> O anything, of nothing first create!
> O heavy lightness, serious vanity,
> Misshapen chaos of well-seeming forms,
> Feather of lead, bright smoke, cold fire, sick health,
> Still-waking sleep, that is not what it is!
>
> -William Shakespeare
> *Romeo & Juliet*
> Romeo; *Act 2, Scene 4*

Misshapen Chaos

Romeo's "Why then…" soliloquy in *Romeo & Juliet* is meant to be confusing. None of those things makes sense. But in this speech, the confusion is intentional; it's a list of metaphors which illustrate the emotional inconsistencies and confusion swirling in Romeo's mind. This soliloquy is his attempt at getting a handle on his own thoughts, but without success; life is making no sense to him, and he can't figure out what to do about it.

When I was teaching — when I was teaching enthusiastically, teaching analytically, teaching above reproach — it was the best time of my life. But now, my life is a cacophony of "misshapen chaos of well-seeming forms."

"Ay me! Sad hours seem long."

Why Then

While you were reading this book, another teacher had an unlawful relationship with a student. And as a result, many school officials across the country are doing what they've always done to prevent this from happening in the future: *Absolutely nothing.*

Why do school officials refuse to take real steps toward solving this problem? Why are schools doing absolutely nothing to address this issue? Clearly it *should* be common sense for teachers *not* to hook up with students, right? However, it isn't exactly working out that way.

Nothing will change as long as school administrators and teachers keep their heads in the sand. Because for every teacher we see on the news, there are two or three teachers who have been dealt with "quietly" and dozens who have flat-out gotten away with it. This is a disease — an epidemic — and no one wants to deal with it, so it is slowly taking its toll.

Don't vow to protect the students while ignoring the very problem that puts them at risk. This *"misshapen chaos of well-seeming forms"* has created the illusion of safety, yet no one can see the fire because of all the smoke.

Serious Vanity

So, just to be perfectly clear: *I do not blame the administration for what I did.* That's pure ridiculousness. I didn't make the choices I made because they didn't tell me not to hook up with a student. However, the time has come for administrators and teachers to be preventative and proactive. The time has come for someone to step forward and state the obvious, because it certainly does not seem to be obvious anymore.

The longer schools ignore this issue, the more teachers we will see on the news with their most recent sex scandal.

Clearly, this is a problem. Yet few schools seem to be doing *anything* to address it.

My choices were my choices — *my fault* — and no one else's. But if I had the chance to say something to someone that would change their perspective and prevent them from making the same choices I did, I would seize that opportunity in a heartbeat. I can't change what I did, but perhaps I can say something or write something which can prevent an instance of this in the future. And if just one teacher changes his/her perspective, it is all worth it.

But that's not what schools want. School administrators think their school is under control. Principals think they've got it handled.

They're wrong.

Still-waking Sleep

EDUCATORS: *Do something* to address this issue! This is happening *in your school,* right now, as you read this sentence. I knew about instances of teacher-student relationships long before I ever crossed that line myself. And I will forever regret not speaking up, because these teachers have gotten away with it and are still teaching. But the established culture among the faculty was clear: "I see nothing; I hear nothing; I know nothing." And I certainly wasn't the only teacher who knew.

That's the key. The culture *as-a-whole* must be changed! And before this can happen, the issue must be pulled from the shadows and thrust into the spotlight at center stage. Make it an issue among the faculty. If it remains a *hush-hush* issue, then it will keep happening in *hush-hush* manners and handled with *hush-hush* "solutions." However, if it becomes a forward and public issue among all faculty, perhaps it will quash the inclinations of teachers who seem to think that a relationship with a student is somehow secretly permissible. Because judging by the number of teachers hitting the news lately, "secretly permissible" seems to be the general perspective, as long as no one gets caught.

It's sad when *someone like me* must be the voice of reason.

Do something about this.

Change the culture.

Be the change.

Now.

EPILOGUE

Mild spring winds always smell like the breeze which encircled me at the end of a long and glorious day of being a teacher. So those are the feelings onto which I choose to grasp in the memories of my mind's eye. There is this feeling, unparalleled by anything, when a teacher walks out of the building at the end of the day knowing he/she has simply and gloriously taught well that day; like a sculptor stepping back from his work, pleased (and a little surprised) at his own abilities. There were literally days when teaching was so much fun, I actually grinned at the notion that I was being paid to do it. And it was all about being a teacher — nothing more.

However, those polluted memories of my after-3PM depravities still (and will always) linger. There is nothing I can do to completely detach my wonderful memories of teaching from my remorseful ones. But I can never take back the affairs I had with my colleagues, the out-of-control teacher parties in which I partook, the secrets I kept, or the choices which led me to prison. So even in my memory's most beautiful sunny days, dark clouds will always linger on the horizon.

I cannot bring myself to drive by my high school. I was a student at that school, I graduated from that school, I taught at that school, I interned at that school, and I disgraced that school. I can never go back; not even for a class reunion. And, in fact, I cannot even drive by it — not because I'm not allowed or anything of the sort, but because I simply can't handle the sight of what has become an architectural reminder of my ruined life. It literally hurts to know what I had, what I ruined, and all the people I hurt along the way.

Obviously, not all teachers are having relationships with students. There really are many great teachers out there who deserve higher pay and more recognition and appreciation. Teaching can often be a thankless profession — financially, professionally, and publicly — so maybe there is a silver-lining to the lack of publicity of the teachers who are having relationships with students. Because honestly, when I was arrested for what I did, I didn't just reflect poorly on myself, I made all teachers and the teaching profession look terrible — thus, I reflected poorly on some amazing educators whose only goal is to nurture and broaden the minds of the future.

I will never realistically have the opportunity to ask their forgiveness.

Turn Around

Every now and then, I fall apart.[184] There is an immeasurable amount of guilt which I carry every single day of my life. I can never take back what I've done and the pain I've caused. I can only turn from what I did and walk — no, *run* — in the opposite direction, doing everything I can to help prevent someone else from making the choices I've made and hurting people the way I hurt those I knew, taught, and loved. And even with every effort I make — every step, every speech, every word written — I still, every now and then, fall apart. It is shocking how a few moments of terrible choices can ruin an entire life, both mine and hers. I carry that guilt with me every minute of every day.

I cannot — *ever* — fix the pain I've caused. But I also cannot sit idly by while I see story after story scroll across the news about the

---

184 Yes, I happened to be listening to this song ("Total Eclipse of the Heart") when I wrote this paragraph. Well, actually, I was watching *Grey's Anatomy* while writing this paragraph, and I heard the version featured on the show by Jill Andrews. It's a very soft, melancholy, and haunting rendition of the song; pretty much the opposite of Adam Sandler's version in *The Wedding Singer*.

latest teacher who had an unlawful relationship with a student. I have an insight which no one else seems to share, likely because they do not want to be the target of further ridicule.[185]

Please don't be me. Please don't let your colleagues be me. Please don't let your friends be me. Please — *please* — do not be me. Living a ruined life is unfathomable. I've heard several people use the expression "putting the pieces back together," but the truth is, there's no such thing. I can't put the pieces back together, because my life is now an incomplete puzzle, never to be reassembled again. I am fortune's fool, and yet, I have no one to blame but myself.

Look at me. Look hard. Because this is what a ruined life looks like.

I have a wonderful future behind me.

---

185 Honestly, this is completely understandable. But I still feel that I owe it to the profession to affect a positive change for the future; penance for the damage I caused in the past.

APPENDIX

Writing a book is no simple task. It's not simply a matter of putting words on a page and handing them over to someone to be put between a front and back cover. And composition is not a simple task either. There is quite a bit involved in the process; much of it can be open to interpretation, and often needs clarification, otherwise the entire point of the book may be lost or convoluted due to errant assumptions by the reader. Thus, in an issue as important as this, clarification is necessary.

Overview

As a former English teacher, I still hold a deep-seeded love for literature and literary theory, so as I wrote this book, I sought to implement as many literary devices and strategies as I could. However, as I distributed early digital and paper copies of this book to numerous "Beta Readers"[186] whose opinions I trust and value, several points were made which I feel necessitate some further explanation (hence, this appendix).

This appendix is not meant to justify, but rather, to clarify and expand, much like watching a DVD with the Director Commentary.

---

186 A "Beta Reader" is essentially a test audience for a book. Writers write, and readers read; but when a writer attempts to read his/her own writing, it can be difficult to catch any unintended errors, confusions, or perceptions which a reader may find with ease. Any writer who does not utilize Beta Readers does so at his/her peril.

Tone

The use of tone in this book is vital because one of my paramount goals was for the reader to understand how the issue of unlawful teacher-student relationships is going somewhat unchecked. Therefore, I felt that a use of a disparaging tone when referring to the manner in which the issue is (and/or is not) being addressed conveyed the sense of overall societal frustration about the issue as a whole.

Additionally, the tone of me as an individual also plays a vital role. For example, several Beta Readers pointed out that the tone I conveyed during my interrogation by the police (cocky, arrogant, defiant) differed greatly from my tone near the end of the book (humble, remorseful, somewhat self-deprecating) which seemed to put the two at odds with one another. This was a conscious choice of style because it illustrates how much I — *as a person* — changed through these experiences. Essentially, reading about my thoughts, actions, and attitude early in the book creates somewhat of an unlikable character. And while I could have gone back and re-edited that section to portray myself as less of a jerk, I wanted to leave it, creating a stark contrast between the person at the beginning of the book and the person at the end — essentially, the positive evolution of the protagonist.

Intentions

The Prologue is also a section which has garnered some questions regarding its purpose. I've been asked several times if the purpose of telling the brief story of the suicide of Donald Blair was an attempt at making the reader feel sorry for him.

No. Not at all.

The story of Donald Blair is an anecdotal example of the emotional impact an unlawful teacher-student relationship has on the teacher — not to create sympathy, but rather, to humanize the situation. While demonizing teachers who have unlawful relationships with students may be appropriate,[187] current teachers who may be on the cusp of

---

187 ...to a certain extent.

this situation need to see something beyond a television mugshot and a humiliating news story. Essentially, relaying the story of Donald Blair was one more way to make the situation a bit more real and human for a teacher reading this book. Don't feel sorry for Donald Blair.[188] But see him in the appropriate context: A man filled with more regret and remorse than he could possibly handle, leading him to take his own life.

Movie References

I reference multiple films in this book. One of my Beta Readers told me she thought the reason I referenced so many movies was because I had trouble distinguishing between fantasy and reality. But the truth is, I'm just a movie buff. I reference movies in my everyday life more often than Anthony DiNozzo. The film references are nothing more than ways to parallel a given point or a certain contextual situation.

Being a fan of films of most genres, quoting films and relating to films is a way for me to enjoy the writing process a bit more, but it is also another writing strategy for relating to readers on a level beyond the text. Chuck Klosterman, my favorite contemporary writer, does the same thing with music and musicians.

Overall Goal

So why write this book? Simple: To keep others from doing what I did, and to help reveal the ones who are doing it. *That's it.* When it comes down to the core purpose of why I spent years writing this book and why I am putting myself into the public eye as someone who committed these horrid crimes, it is because I possess within me a drive to remedy this problem in the future, having seen the damage and pain it has caused in the past.

---

188 ...or me, for that matter.

Not to get overly-spiritual, but if I were a Christian,[189] I'd estimate that this was God's purpose for me, enduring life experiences in order to benefit others in the future. That is — for the most part — the "why" of this book. I feel that I have been given an opportunity by a higher power to make a positive difference; and since God has bestowed upon me the gift of being a writer, then I must use it to the best of my ability for something good. Because, in the words of the legendary Steve Prefontaine, "To give anything less than your best is to sacrifice the gift."

---

189 …which I am, or, at least, I'm trying.

ACKNOWLEDGEMENTS

The author would like to acknowledge and thank the following individuals for their support and inspiration in the writing of this book:

- My wife, who stood by me, even though I gave her every reason to leave — she is my proof that God exists.
- My family and friends who continued to believe I wasn't an evil person, regardless of the evil things I've done.
- The "family" and "friends" who disowned me: You were just as much an inspiration to change my life as anyone.
- My attorney, Jess Hoeme of *Joseph, Hollander, & Craft* in Wichita, who went above-and-beyond in his defense of me — if not for him, I would have done twice as much time in prison.
- My friends and family who helped proofread and edit the many pieces of this manuscript, from its preconception to its release date.
- Chuck and Tommy, who refused to judge me by my choices before prison, and instead, judged me by who I was *after* prison.
- Rob, for being a shining example of how to stand up to critics, haters, and naysayers while maintaining class, dignity, and respect.
- Aubrey, David, and the rest of the team at Morgan James Publishing, who believed enough in *After 3PM*, to take a chance on me and offer me my first book deal.
- Most of all, God, for *not* giving me what I truly deserved.

The most beautiful things in the world are the things that are shattered, broken, and then mended back together.

-John Cusack

ABOUT THE AUTHOR

Kurt Michael Brundage, M.Ed. is an author and former high school teacher. He holds bachelor's degrees in English and psychology as well as a master's degree in school administration. Beginning in 2012, he spent 25 months in prison after having a brief relationship with a former student. He now works as a writer, public  speaker, and activist, addressing the issue of unlawful teacher-student relationships by speaking to teachers, future teachers, and school officials and giving teacher trainings on the epidemic of unlawful teacher-student relationships. Kurt, his wife, and his daughter live in Wichita, Kansas.

www.kurtbrundage.com

Morgan James
Speakers Group

➤ www.TheMorganJamesSpeakersGroup.com

We connect Morgan James published
authors with live and online events
and audiences who will benefit
from their expertise.

CPSIA information can be obtained
at www.ICGtesting.com
Printed in the USA
BVHW03s0048290318
511921BV00001B/18/P

9 781683 506836